SILENT
SOULS
WEEPING

SILENT SOULS WEEPING

DEPRESSION

Sharing Stories
Finding Hope

JANE CLAYSON JOHNSON

DESERET
BOOK

SALT LAKE CITY, UTAH

Library of Congress Cataloging-in-Publication Data

Names: Johnson, Jane Clayson, author.
Title: Silent souls weeping : depression-sharing stories, finding hope / Jane Clayson Johnson.
Description: Salt Lake City, Utah : Deseret Book, [2018] | Includes bibliographical references.
Identifiers: LCCN 2018039977 | ISBN 9781629725253 (hardbound : alk. paper)
Subjects: LCSH: Depression, Mental—Religious aspects—The Church of Jesus Christ of Latter-day Saints. | Depression, Mental—Religious aspects—Mormon Church. | The Church of Jesus Christ of Latter-day Saints—Doctrines. | Mormon Church— Doctrines.
Classification: LCC BX8643.D44 J64 2018 | DDC 248.8/625—dc23
LC record available at https://lccn.loc.gov/2018039977

Printed in the United States of America
Lake Book Manufacturing, Inc., Melrose Park, IL

10   9   8   7   6   5   4   3   2   1

So my children will understand

CONTENTS

CHAPTER 1

DEPRESSION IN THE FIRST PERSON: MY STORY

*Why art thou cast down, O my soul? and
why art thou disquieted in me?*

—PSALM 42:5

N ot long ago, my daughter and I attended an Easter performance at a church in Nashua, New Hampshire. During the intermission I ran into an old friend, a chirpy, optimistic, upbeat soul I've always loved for her candor and authenticity. We immediately started chatting and catching up on our busy lives and growing families. At one point she asked, "So, tell me, what's new with you? What are you up to these days?"

"Well, I'm writing another book," I replied. And then I just spit it out, without thinking: "About depression." Her eyes widened in surprise. "Really?" she said. I could practically see the wheels turning in her mind, and then she asked, "*You* don't have depression . . . *do you?*"

When I started this project I wasn't so direct. I may have worried a little that someone would ask that very question. This is not a book I ever expected to write. To be frank, I grew up with the notion that mental illness is not something to discuss. Ever. I'd bought into the stigma associated with it. After all, we believe in a plan of happiness, not a plan of depression. We're taught, "Men are, that they might have joy" (2 Nephi 2:25). Depression doesn't fit readily or comfortably into such a construct.

I want to be clear: I am not a doctor or a therapist. My experience

1

with depression is personal and observational, not scientific. Although I have consulted experts, my intention is not to diagnose anyone or to offer any sort of treatment plan, and this book is not a self-help guide to overcoming depression and mental illness.

I also want to be clear that this book is limited in its scope; it offers many individual insights into the lives of depression sufferers, while saying little or nothing about some very important aspects of this illness. For example, it is known that the elderly are increasingly susceptible to depression as they age and often become more homebound and isolated, but I did not delve into the experience of that specific population.

Likewise, there is only token acknowledgment of the high levels of depression in the LGBTQ+ community. My intention is to call attention to the struggle—the rejection, isolation, stigmatization— while in no way suggesting that there is a direct correlation between being gay, for example, and experiencing elevated levels of depression as a clinical illness. Members of our LGBTQ+ population often do not feel embraced theologically or accepted culturally into the Latter-day Saint community. I seek to highlight that being marginalized or rejected, regardless of cause, aggravates depression—the greater the isolation, the more extreme the risk of serious, even life-threatening emotional health problems. This is a subject of great complexity, needing a book of its own.

So, rather than being a comprehensive view of all aspects of depression, this work is simply my effort to raise the blinds on the windows of a darkened room and talk openly about what it means to be depressed—specifically what it feels like for members of The Church of Jesus Christ of Latter-day Saints to suffer from diseases of the mind. It's also a primer to help educate those who are spared this challenge. I want to offer hope and encouragement *and* urge us all to action. There are precious souls stranded in the wilderness of this affliction needing our rescue.

For the past three years, I've put my journalism skills to use and spent every spare minute researching, interviewing, and writing the stories of Latter-day Saints who have depression and other mental illnesses. This book is a collection of those experiences, along with a few of my own. I hope it will become a means for all members of the Church—whether they suffer from depression themselves or love someone who does—to set aside their preconceived notions about mental illness and be more "willing to bear one another's burdens, that they may be light . . . and . . . mourn with those that mourn . . . and comfort those that stand in need of comfort" (Mosiah 18:8–9).

Although in my own circle of acquaintance I am most familiar with the emotional challenges faced by Latter-day Saint women, I have interviewed broadly in the hopes that all—men and women, adults and youth, priesthood leaders and those who minister under their direction—will find relatable stories and examples that can be helpfully applied to their own situations. My desire is that this book will launch conversations within families, between friends, in Church settings such as Relief Society and priesthood meetings, and between Church members and their ecclesiastical shepherds, conversations that will improve understanding and the quality of the ministering we offer as a result.

MY STORY

Abraham Lincoln, arguably one of the most influential men of the nineteenth century, experienced several documented periods of deep depression. At one point, he wrote to a friend: "I am now the most miserable man living. If what I feel were equally distributed to the whole human family, there would not be one cheerful face on earth. Whether I shall ever be better, I cannot tell; I awfully forbode I shall not. To remain as I am is impossible."

3

I can't think of a better way to describe how I felt during the worst of my own depression. Thankfully, I no longer feel this way. But I understand; the experience of depression is excruciating.

Over the years, I had experienced small, contained bouts of what I call "situational sadness." Nothing serious—just the ups and downs of life. Nothing a good cry (or two or three) couldn't fix. It wasn't until I was finally living my dream of being a wife and a mother to five children (two of my own and three stepchildren) that the insidious fingers of mental illness wrapped themselves around my mind and squeezed. Tight.

Before I was clinically diagnosed with major depressive disorder, unexpected illness and physical changes took my body for a long, hard ride. A couple of years after the birth of my second child, I began to acknowledge that something wasn't quite right. I was chronically agitated and irritated and simply didn't feel well. I cried a lot. I was tired all the time; I could sleep ten to twelve hours and wake up exhausted. I reminded myself I was a harried, not-so-young mother with young children; what did I expect? My doctor adjusted my thyroid medication. It made no difference at all.

I was approaching forty, and we were racing the biological clock to try to have one more child. It wasn't happening. I'll never forget the day I went to Brigham and Women's Hospital in Boston for a follow-up appointment with a fertility specialist. Having completed the initial, exhaustive round of screenings and blood panels, I was quite confident that Dr. Ginsburg would prescribe an easy fix—maybe some hormones to stimulate ovulation—and send me on my way. Instead, she delivered devastating news: "You have premature ovarian failure."

As it turned out, I was in full-blown menopause. The difficult and complicated surgery I'd undergone to deliver my son at twenty-seven weeks gestation had done irreversible damage. I would not have another child.

But I wasn't ready to give up, so I chased down a specialist who put me through several different rounds of hormone-replacement therapy. These did nothing to help me conceive, but they did trigger massive migraine cycles that flattened me for days at a time. I felt like my body was shutting down. On top of everything else, depression was making itself at home.

I managed to function at a bare minimum; I had a family to care for and Church responsibilities to fulfill. But I was right on the edge of an abyss. Frequently, and without warning, horribly negative emotions would flood my mind. Darkness. Gloom. Cruel and damaging internal monologues. By turns, I felt numb and deadened, angry and volatile. Who was this person? It was like a switch was being toggled in my brain: Dr. Jekyll, Mr. Hyde. It frightened me. My husband and kids bore the brunt of my erratic moods. And then the guilt would set in—a terrible cycle. I was ashamed of my behavior and horrified by what I was feeling. And so I didn't talk about it—with anyone.

I began to isolate myself. My world became a very solitary place because I just wanted to be left alone. I routinely made excuses to avoid Relief Society activities or invitations to dinner with friends. Inevitably, Sunday would come and I'd make myself go to church, forcing a smile through gritted teeth. I didn't feel uplifted, and I was certain no one would understand my struggle. I would avoid talking to anyone, hurry out as quickly as I could, and fall into bed for much of the rest of the day.

I accused myself of being ungrateful. How could I be so depressed when I was so blessed? To those around me, it must have seemed like I had it all: a loving, righteous husband, beautiful children, professional success. I worked extremely hard to maintain that veneer of normalcy. The truth was, beneath the seemingly successful surface lay a bleak void, as abnormal as anything I could imagine.

Perhaps most distressing was what was happening to my testimony.

For long stretches of time, I couldn't feel the Spirit. I did the right things: said my prayers, read my scriptures, and went to the temple. But I didn't *feel* anything. It was as if the most important part of my soul had been carved out of me. Why would God do that to me? Why would He allow it?

All my life, whether in the most stressful and strenuous times at work or the most painful passages at home, I've stayed strong. I am a believer. I fight for my faith. I always want God to know that He can trust me. In any situation, I am definitively on the Lord's side. He knows it. I know it. But in this time of torment, He seemed unresponsive to my pleadings. Why had He abandoned me?

As my cycles of shame, guilt, and anger intensified, the self-criticism in my head became more insistent and insidious. "I have failed my family." "My children would be so much better off with a different mother." "My husband deserves more than this." I concluded it would be better for everyone if I weren't around. I didn't have a plan or mechanism for making these thoughts reality. I just daydreamed about falling asleep and fading away. It was a resigned hopelessness. And every day, I knew I was drawing closer to an end.

It truly felt impossible to continue in that state. In my mind, I began planning my funeral: deciding who would speak, choosing the music and hymns, visualizing the flowers and the chapel full of people. I knew that I wanted to be buried under the drooping branches of a willow tree. As nonsensical as this sounds to me now, at the time it seemed completely rational. I felt broken and worthless. In my mind, I needed to protect my family from my shortcomings and failures.

THE REPLACEMENT

The most urgent item on my mental to-do list was finding my "replacement." Silently, secretly, I began to search for a new mother for my children, a new wife for my husband. This angelic soul would be the kind of person I had convinced myself I could never be: patient, kind, easygoing, even-tempered, noncritical, a woman who would certainly never scream at her kids. Anyone, really, would be a better mother and wife than I was.

I remember feeling genuine relief when I finally identified her: a delightful, engaging, smart, and unmarried young woman. I'll call her Sarah. She was spiritually sensitive and mature. Lovely and kind. I started asking her to babysit my kids on occasion so she could get to know them. I wanted them to be comfortable with her, too. Then one night I found the courage to ask her if she would take over my life.

Of course, Sarah had no idea that I sometimes wished my life would end. And I had no idea that just around the bend there was a light at the end of this very dark tunnel.

I'll jump ahead to the conversation I had with Sarah when I tracked her down several years after the preceding events occurred. I asked for her perspective on what happened that night.

JANE: "Do you remember the conversation where I said to you, in a very roundabout way, that if I was ever 'not around,' I wanted you to adopt my children because you'd be such an amazing mother? Do you remember that?"

SARAH: "I remember it very clearly. You told me how much you loved your children. And you kept complimenting me on how well I interacted with them. You also told me that if anything ever happened to you, you wanted me to marry Mark and raise them."

JANE: "What was your reaction to that?"

SARAH: "I remember thinking, 'What am I supposed to feel right now? Am I supposed to be flattered? Should I be concerned?' I remember mostly just being puzzled. I've thought about it many times since. Do you remember how the conversation started?"

7

JANE: "No, I don't."

SARAH: "You pulled out a bunch of clothes from your closet. You told me how much you had loved wearing them, but you thought that they would look great—or better, you said—on me. It's interesting, because in the years since that happened I've dealt with mental illness issues in my own family and with friends. I was younger then. I now recognize those signs . . . and I've wondered if it were to happen again, if my reaction would be different."

Nothing else really happened that afternoon with Sarah. I didn't outright ask her to take my children. She declined to take any of my clothes. The weeks went on, and the depression persisted. My husband grew increasingly concerned. I remember him praying specifically for my health. On my birthday he sent me to a spa, suggesting that a little "alone time" and some pampering would help. He curtailed his grueling travel schedule and increasingly bore the load of a busy home life. But still, he really had little intimation of the intensity of my feelings.

WATCHCARE IN THE WOODS

A number of weeks later, on a Sunday afternoon, in a state of complete despair, I drove about an hour from my home and just sat in my car, reclined the seat, and cried. My husband was frantically calling me, trying to find me. I turned off my phone. I didn't know what to do. I was feeling emotions I'd never experienced before, and they terrified me. After I had been sitting there for several hours, a man on a walk around the woods passed my car and knocked on the window, asking if I was okay. Certainly he could see I was crying and upset. I remember he had such kind eyes. He asked if there were anything he could do to help. I replied no, thank you.

He said something like, "It's getting dark. Do you have someone you can call just to talk?" I rolled up the window and called Mark. We talked and talked and talked. He convinced me to come home . . . that he needed me. And then he just took over. The next morning, first thing, he called my physician. He stayed with me around the clock for several days. He took me to two different doctors.

I was diagnosed with major depressive disorder. The doctors persuaded me that my children didn't need a new mother. My husband didn't need a new wife. They needed *me*—the *real* me, not this person whose mind had been hijacked by illness. I started taking an antidepressant and seeing a cognitive behavioral therapist. Little by little at the start, and then more quickly, the chains began to loosen.

Before I started taking medication, I felt as though I'd reached the top of a very steep flight of stairs. Another set of stairs was just ahead of me, but it was out of my reach. If I tried to put my foot on that higher step, all the stairs would collapse and turn into a slide of sorts, hurtling me down. When the medicine began to work, it was as though another step appeared. I was able to move forward and keep climbing as I utilized the tools I needed to heal. With each step, more and more hope returned. The darkness lifted, and so did the numbness. Increasingly I felt like myself again. Peace illuminated the horizon.

"I THOUGHT I WAS THE ONLY ONE"

As my mind cleared, my empathy grew. I had been so alone in the depths of that depression, and I felt a need to share. Tentatively at first, and always in safe settings—with a friend over lunch or during a visit at home—I began to tell others about my experience. What happened was remarkable. As I told my story, others shared theirs with me. I heard about similar experiences from people who had suffered with all sorts of mental illnesses—some for weeks, months, even years.

Then, on October 5, 2013, I heard these words from Elder Jeffrey R. Holland, a man called as an Apostle of God:

"Today I am speaking of . . . an affliction so severe that it significantly restricts a person's ability to function fully, a crater in the mind so deep that no one can responsibly suggest it would surely go away if those victims would just square their shoulders and think more positively.

" . . . I once terrifyingly saw it in myself. At one point in our married life when financial fears collided with staggering fatigue, I took a psychic blow that was as unanticipated as it was real. With the grace of God and the love of my family, I kept functioning and kept working, but even after all these years I continue to feel a deep sympathy for others more chronically or more deeply afflicted with such gloom than I was. In any case we have all taken courage from those who, in the words of the Prophet Joseph, 'search[ed] . . . and contemplate[d] the darkest abyss' and persevered through it—not the least of whom were Abraham Lincoln, Winston Churchill, and Elder George Albert Smith, the latter being one of the most gentle and Christlike men of our dispensation, who battled recurring depression for some years before becoming the universally beloved eighth prophet and President of The Church of Jesus Christ of Latter-day Saints."

This was a watershed moment for me, a moment I have since wanted to extend and explore until, as Elder Holland proclaimed, each person who suffers from this debilitating plague can break through the fog and stigma of depression and latch on to the hope of recovery:

"Though we may feel we are 'like a broken vessel,' as the Psalmist says, we must remember, that vessel is in the hands of the divine potter. *Broken minds can be healed just the way broken bones and broken hearts are healed.*"

After my own broken mind healed, I felt a measure of assertiveness return to me, the same assertiveness that had played such a huge part in my career. The journalist in me took over. Instead of just talking to people, I asked to interview them. In the end, I had interviewed more than 150 women, men, teenagers, and children—all faithful members of the Church who had suffered in silence while depression declared war on their brains. I catalogued and categorized those conversations—qualitative data, one PhD informed me—and tried to identify trends and themes in the interviews, drawing a map through what I heard.

Many of these people were initially strangers whom I cold-called after a friend or a previous interviewee provided their names and numbers. I explained my objectives, my mission for this book, and usually within a few minutes we would settle into an intimate conversation about their experiences. I heard repeatedly, "I've never talked about this with anyone." Or, "My parents don't even know this." Or, "I'm kind of surprised I'm telling you this." Most remarkable is that, on several occasions, people I did not know called *me*. "I hear you're writing a book about mental illness; can I tell you my story?" Some women brought me their journals. Others wrote pages of thoughts and remembrances and had their spouses do the same. It struck me that people wanted to be heard. They needed their experiences to be validated. And they desperately wished to help others who suffer. These exchanges went on for more than a year. Gradually, by fits and starts, and with more struggle than I can describe, this book began to take shape.

Some days I became so overwhelmed with the sheer volume of information—and suffering—that I considered abandoning my project. I had collected thousands of pages of transcripts and research—it was like drinking from a fire hose. Everyone's stories were personal and profound, and I felt tremendous responsibility and stewardship for the information that had been entrusted to me. I couldn't do it justice. But then I would talk to someone else and see their eyes light up when I mentioned the book I was writing and what I hoped it could do. I would take another step forward.

I hope you'll agree that this is a conversation we need to have. Many Latter-day Saints have mastered the challenge of caring for others who find themselves battling poor physical health, drowning in financial trials, or dealing with the loss of a loved one. We must also learn to muster the same compassion, love, understanding, and help for those who suffer ailments of the mind. Charity, not judgment, is the balm we should offer. Almost all of us, I believe, want to be like the concerned gentleman rambling through the woods who came to my aid in a moment of crisis. We want to lift the downcast and succor the weak. Be an answer to a loved one's prayer. Sustain a fellow traveler when the road becomes unspeakably daunting. We yearn to be like Jesus, discerning the unspoken need and offering our shoulders to help lighten the burdens others carry, regardless of their cause.

The worst part of depression is the profound isolation it engenders, not just from the Spirit but from family, friends, and community. Early on in my research, I held a focus group at my home with a group of women I'd known for years, and with whom, together and separately, I had discussed literature, parenting, Church callings, politics, you name it. But until that evening, we had not shared with each other our struggles with mental illness, whether our own or those of loved ones. We talked into the night. It was a remarkably honest and healing exchange. The next day, one of the women who had opened up about her own depression emailed me saying that in the seven years we'd been meeting she'd never felt as close to the women in our group as she had the previous night.

She said she felt different after that conversation. She had exposed herself, but also—for the first time—felt like others understood what she was going through; she was not alone in her pain. "Hearing one another's struggles made me feel like we were on sacred ground," she told me.

That revelation was a beginning. As the great Christian theologian and author C. S. Lewis once wrote, "Friendship is born at that moment when one person says to another: 'What! You too? I thought I was the only one.'" This undertaking has been replete with those "What! You too?" moments. As I've shared my story and listened in return to complete strangers and lifelong friends as they told me theirs, I've been humbled, had my heart broken again and again, and discovered hope through the Savior's Atonement that is brighter and more all-encompassing than I could ever have imagined.

CHAPTER 2

"O God,
Where Art Thou?"

*O God, where art thou? And where is the
pavilion that covereth thy hiding place?*

—Doctrine and Covenants 121:1

Janna's first experience with clinical depression sprang out of nowhere. It had been years since her family had experienced a significant trauma or heartbreak. Her husband had a good job, her four kids were healthy and happy, and they lived minutes from some of the most beautiful beaches in the country. "I should have been living it up," she says. "Instead I was barely living."

Her one big trial at the time was her eighteen-month-old son, who still didn't sleep for more than two or three hours at a time. Janna attributed her moodiness and frequent tears to sleep deprivation. But six months later, when she and her son were both finally sleeping through the night, the haze hadn't lifted. Her mood swings had leveled out . . . in the wrong direction. She was now mostly irritable rather than not. Her tears had been replaced with an odd numbness and incessant, negative self-talk.

"The numbness was a lack of feeling, really, something akin to apathy," Janna says. "The best example I can give now is that during this time I was waiting for my first book to be published. On the day that a box of fifty of my freshly printed books arrived at my house, I opened it up with the same enthusiasm you'd use to open up a package of socks or my monthly Amazon delivery of laundry detergent and diapers. I simply didn't care that I was now a published author. I felt no excitement whatsoever that I was holding a beautiful copy of my very own book in my hands."

Janna also recalls a sense of frantic desperation. "I prayed constantly for help, for relief from the exhaustion, for just the smallest bit of energy so that I could feel like myself again. That I could feel anything, to be honest. But I just kept hitting a wall. I felt anything but normal. By the time that box was delivered, I had settled into a place where I was doing only the bare minimum. I'd started finding ways to get out of social activities, I retreated to my bed as frequently as I could, and I found my mind filled with negative thoughts. I was convinced that my former self was lost, never to return. And that I deserved it."

Sundays were her most difficult days. Her husband was serving as the bishop, so she would get the kids ready for church on her own, sneak in a few minutes late, and sink into a bench in the chapel, feeling completely mystified that no one else had noticed the dark cloud trailing after her. "I came to church during those months convinced that I was a hypocrite and terrified that others were going to catch on. I felt like all of my prayers were hitting a brick wall. It had been ages since I'd felt the Spirit. Surely it was a sign that I was unworthy. I'll never forget the Sunday that we found a spot to sit on the second row, directly in front of the seats where the bishopric sits. I was feeling nothing that day. Nothing. I looked up at my husband, who had just sat down after speaking. He was looking a little misty eyed, as was nearly everyone around me. It was clear that the rest of the congregation had just witnessed a powerful testimony. I don't think I had ever felt more alone than in that moment, when I felt certain that I had lost not just the *ability* to feel the Spirit but the privilege of being *worthy* to feel it."

Dozens of metaphors have been used to describe depression, but none do it justice. There is simply no way to convey the intensity of a major depressive episode without resorting to words like strangling, drowning, choking, sinking, and suffocating. Its physical symptoms—headaches, fatigue, intestinal distress—are mild when compared to its effects on the mind and spirit. In his award-winning book, *The Noonday Demon: An Atlas of Depression,* Andrew Solomon describes it as "the arid pain of total violation that comes after the tears are all used up, the pain that stops up every space through which you once metered the world, or the world, you."

Depression is difficult to describe even when you've experienced it yourself. And for each person who suffers with it, a new description is written. Here are a few examples from my interviews:

MEGHAN: "I felt so guilty and so dark and just like there's something wrong with me. I can't function in my life."

LIZ: "I just kind of flatlined. I couldn't get mad, couldn't get upset, couldn't do anything. Just kind of went through everything in a fog. Depression manifests itself very differently with people. . . . I wasn't crying, and I wasn't suicidal. I just couldn't feel anything. That's depression too. . . . I have described it as there being a veil between me and the rest of the world. Very gauzy, but a veil. I'm just not fully present."

MATTEUS: "We have ADD in our family and depression. In me, when you put ADD and depression together, you get a lot of anger, and I was really . . . I was just a poor anger manager when I was a young father. I'd blow my stack at my kids, and then I'd be so embarrassed. I'd think, 'I've got to get someone to help me with this. But who do I explain this to? They'll never believe me because I'm the nicest person who was ever born.'"

ERISHA: "When I am deeply, darkly depressed, I feel like it's shaken all of my spiritual foundations because I can't feel anything the way

I used to feel it. There are ways that depression manifests itself that some of us are more comfortable sharing, and ways that it manifests itself that seem to hit deeply at the core, foundationally, of who we are, what we believe, and what we've built our life around. I think sometimes it's easy to share, 'I'm depressed. I'm in bed. I'm sad.' But saying, 'I'm depressed; I want to walk out on my children,' that's a different thing."

DAVID: "First of all, it's really a deep, blue, dark, completely hopeless mood where doing even the smallest things just really required a ton of effort. It was hard to even get out of bed in the morning. I had no motivation to do anything. I had no interest in things I used to have interest in. I ended up just feeling completely empty. There was this awful emptiness."

SARIAH: "Depression makes you feel so disconnected. You feel like God has abandoned you completely. You feel so estranged, so severed from His Spirit that you think, 'Why is this happening? Why am I abandoned; what did I do wrong?'"

WILL: "I have done everything I could possibly do in the last four years, I think, to be worthy and deserving of the Lord's blessing because I want that so much. I say this in my prayers sometimes, 'Lord, I don't understand. There's supposed to be the joy of the Saints. There's supposed to be the peace of the gospel, and I'm doing everything that I know, and yet I'm not feeling joy or peace.'"

ANNE: "Not only do I feel I can't help myself, my husband can't help me, my mother can't help me, but I feel God can't help me either. It's just this feeling of abject loneliness mixed with a pretty heavy dose of, 'And I'm unlovable. If He could help me, He wouldn't. If He did love me, I wouldn't be experiencing this depression.' It's that cyclical experience as well. . . . You're sort of feeling pain on the one hand but a lack of emotion on the other hand. It's sort of an inability to feel

17

and yet an oversensitivity to sadness or this black cloud of melancholy that comes."

As depression encroaches, it does, indeed, change how you think about and perceive everything around you. From the dark depths of the disease it seems that previous sources of pleasure and satisfaction have been cut away. The book lover no longer enjoys a good summer read. Music that previously soothed the soul or thrilled the heart barely registers. Thoughts scatter, distraction destroys focus, and feelings of worthlessness and hopelessness distort perspective. Access to the divine feels blocked. For me, and for many of the Latter-day Saints I interviewed, the latter is the most distressing symptom of depression. It's also one of the most shocking because of our doctrine that the Holy Ghost can be a constant companion. What does it mean, many wonder, when that promised comfort seems beyond reach?

As Dr. James MacArthur, former mission president and former director of the BYU Counseling Center in Provo, Utah, says: "When you are depressed, believing you have failed at something regularly referred to as 'the plan of happiness' can very quickly generate despair."

Much of the research surrounding depression and other mental illnesses is focused on the physical and, specifically, the chemical makeup of the brain and how its functions (and malfunctions) affect our minds and bodies. But depression's spiritual symptoms are just as real. In Doctrine and Covenants 88:15, we are taught that "The spirit and the body are the soul of man." The two are inextricably linked: what affects the body also affects the spirit.

Dr. Louise Jorgensen, a licensed clinical mental-health counselor and board member of the Association of Mormon Counselors and Psychotherapists, uses a great metaphor to explain what is happening when a depressed person feels like they've been spiritually exiled.

Think of the design of a typical home. Wires run through the walls connecting the appliances, heating apparatuses, cooling systems, and so on to the electrical current delivered from a power station far away. The electrical current is steady, but when an aberration causes the current to jump too high—perhaps too many appliances are running at once—a circuit breaker cuts off the power in that part of the house. The current is still coming in, but it's been temporarily interrupted. A home with a tripped breaker hasn't lost its access to electricity; likewise, the depressed person who can no longer feel the Spirit isn't without the Spirit.

"Depression," Dr. Jorgensen says, "leads to a tripping of our circuit breakers. So the power's still trying to get through. God does not stop talking to us, but we can't feel it because our breakers have shut down."

There are physiological reasons why this kind of breakdown happens. The system within your body that helps regulate your reaction to stress as well as your moods and emotions includes a component known as the Hypothalmic-Pituitary-Adrenal Axis, or HPA Axis. The HPA Axis is a type of communication or feedback system between the hypothalamus and pituitary glands—located in the brain—and the adrenal glands, which are just above the kidneys. Dr. Jorgensen explains that these "glands are always talking to each other biochemically to determine what's true and what's tripe." As they communicate and make sense of the messages received and sent, they activate different systems within the body to respond.

One role of the HPA Axis is to help us determine if something is a threat. "From a gospel perspective," Dr. Jorgensen says, this is very interesting because it means "our Heavenly Father placed something in our brains—a system—that indicates to us we are under threat and that this isn't safe and something needs to happen." In the distant past, those threats were often physical. When hunting, for example, the HPA Axis might heighten our sense of hearing so we are better able to identify danger nearby. Generally, however, we no longer need to worry about running into beasts in the wild, she says. "We don't have a lot of external threats anymore. Our threats are more internal, and they can come from the way we think."

In fact, she says, "Scientists now know that there is no difference between a perceived threat and a real threat." We experience both in the same way. This means that if, while hiking, you encountered a rubber rattlesnake placed on the trail and you perceived it to be real, your reaction would be the same as if there were an actual rattlesnake on the trail. Apply this to our thoughts and feelings, and it's easy to see how the feedback cycle can become negative. "People believe things about themselves and the world around them that may not be true," Dr. Jorgensen says. "And when we begin to incorporate those things into our mind and into our life, the HPA Axis begins to go into overdrive. . . . If it gets stuck there long enough, it leads to depression."

When the feedback system provided by the HPA Axis gets stuck in overdrive, detachment or dissociation from reality occurs, numbing the depressed person to positive and even negative emotions. This numbness is like the tripping of the circuit breakers, which cuts off the person's ability to feel the Spirit, along with many other emotions.

Whether they are in our homes or our bodies, those circuits can be reset. When they are in our bodies, the challenge is to press forward despite the despair resulting from being in this situation. The happy news is that, without exception, every person I interviewed *had* forged ahead and learned to maneuver through subsequent depressive episodes, knowing that feeling the loss of the Spirit is a symptom of the disease, not reality and certainly not a permanent condition. The four individuals I highlight here are representative of that. Their stories don't offer a *cure* for depression, but they do provide a reassuring sampling of how a depressed person can press on when the circuits in the brain are preventing the Spirit of the Lord from flowing freely.

SHARING YOUR BURDEN BY SHARING YOUR STORY: A CONVERSATION WITH ROBERT L. MILLET

Robert L. Millet has written beautifully about his experience with a clinical depression "so severe that I simply could not be comforted." The former dean of Religious Education at Brigham Young University, Dr. Millet is one of the most respected minds in religious academia. He holds a master's degree in psychology and a PhD in religious studies; he was also one of my favorite college professors.

For all his vast erudition, his insights into depression are mostly derived from his personal experience with it. He told me:

"When I was first in Church leadership and someone came to me with depression, I would smile and I would try to be compassionate, but inside I was thinking, 'Oh, get off it. Just tighten your belt. Good grief, life is tough.' Until it hit me."

He now describes it as a completely "different ball game" and a "terribly important" subject we need to discuss more in the Church.

"When depression first hit me, I found myself feeling absolutely incapable of doing much of anything. The smallest thing seemed like a mountain to me. If I had been asked to give the closing prayer in a meeting, I would have probably said, 'I'm not sure.'"

Millet was a stake president at the time, and he ultimately counseled with Elder Jeffrey R. Holland about his struggle. Elder Holland never questioned Brother Millet's effectiveness or his ability to serve. Instead, he offered advice to the struggling leader and reminded him frequently that this was an illness that, like other chronic diseases, requires a specific regimen of care and medication to keep at bay.

"[Elder Holland] came over to my house one Sunday afternoon

and he said to me, 'Turn everything over to your counselors. Take as long as you need.' I got this wonderful letter from the First Presidency basically saying the same thing. 'Please take the time to do what you need to do. *Do exactly what your doctors say, and turn everything over to your counselors.*'"

This is a notable example of how any Church leader, in any calling, could accommodate those who have been diagnosed with depression. Unfortunately, this approach is rare in the midst of a culture—both inside and outside the Church—that stigmatizes depression and refuses to recognize it as a real illness. That stigma, paired with the feelings of numbness and worthlessness that accompany depression, can make for a dangerous mix. I asked Brother Millet about this stigma.

JANE: "Is there something specific to our Latter-day Saint culture that makes the issue of mental illness particularly difficult?"

MILLET: "I don't know what all the reasons are, but [many members] somehow feel they're spiritually weak or that their faith in Jesus Christ is not deep enough. Because we believe . . . we know that, 'If you just turn it over to the Savior, He'll handle it.'

"That's easy to hear, but I remember one of the things that was so startling to me was . . . I didn't feel the Spirit in the same way. I just didn't. There's no question in my mind that our mental state and our emotional state can affect our spiritual state.

"Depression affected me in ways I hadn't anticipated. It just made me feel like I couldn't handle anything. Everything seemed overwhelming. And I just wasn't feeling the Spirit of the Lord in the same way."

This paralleled my own experience when depressed. I had wrestled with the paradox that the one thing that had always been present in my life and carried me through many previous trials now seemed completely absent. Wasn't constant access to the Spirit part of the gift given after baptism, at confirmation? I was particularly troubled when I thought of the scripture in Galatians 5:22, in which Paul teaches that the fruits of the Spirit are love, joy, and peace. When depressed, I felt none of that, which generated a great deal of guilt and anxiety that I had driven the Spirit away.

JANE: "What do you tell people who say, 'Well, the fruit of the Spirit is joy and love and peace, and I don't feel any of that, so God must not love me? I must not be . . . '"

MILLET: "I must be in sin?"

JANE: "Exactly! How do you reconcile that?"

MILLET: "In John, chapter 3, where Jesus is talking to Nicodemus, He says, 'The wind blows where it will. You hear the sound, but you can't tell where it's coming from or where it's going.' Then He says, 'So is every one that is born of the Spirit.' We don't always feel the Spirit in the same way. Sometimes we feel it powerfully. You know when someone gets up and just weeps like crazy in a testimony meeting because they are so deeply moved, and you find yourself saying, 'I don't feel anything right now. I don't feel any great spirit'? You're not sinful in this case. You're just not feeling it right then."

Brother Millet shared a particularly poignant story about a young woman he met after he'd given a talk to a group of institute students. She was an institute officer, and the institute director had described her as having "just an amazing spirit." But she was feeling anything but amazing.

MILLET: "I sat with her and she was everything the institute director had said. She was pure, and beautiful, and kind, and sweet. And then she began to describe her depression. I felt I should stop her . . . and

I said, 'Have there been occasions when you just didn't feel like you could feel the Spirit of the Lord?'

"She broke down and began to weep. She said, 'Why?' I said, 'Because that's what I felt.' Suddenly, I could see the burden lift. I saw her shoulders perk up. I quite literally saw a burden lifted from her. This young woman had concluded that clearly she must be doing something wrong spiritually. It was heartbreaking. The institute director said she began to make progress from that point on. Isn't that interesting? Just someone sharing a similar experience—in this case, saying 'it's okay to have depression; it doesn't mean you're a sinner'— can help."

I love that! Just sharing a similar experience can help. It's true!

That sharing is one of the reasons talk therapy can be such a critical part of a successful treatment regimen for depression. Those who courageously share their feelings with a counselor, a friend, or a trusted adviser, such as the young institute officer did with Brother Millet, are able to expose one of the lies circling through their thought processes. It's a lie the adversary loves and certainly hopes we will buy into: that each of us must suffer in solitude. The authentic connection you make when you share your story, and feel it resonate with another's, shatters this lie, bringing hope, comfort, and confirmation that your suffering is real and you are not alone.

A crucial part of talk therapy is storytelling, whether you are simply keeping a record of your negative and positive feelings in a daily log or sharing them with someone else. A recent article in *Psychology Today* reports that "telling your story—while being witnessed with loving attention by others who care—may be the most powerful medicine on earth. . . .

"Every time you tell your story and someone else who cares bears witness to it, you turn off the body's stress responses, flipping off toxic stress hormones like cortisol and epinephrine and flipping on relaxation responses that release healing hormones like oxytocin, do-pamine, nitric oxide, and endorphins. Not only does this turn on the body's innate self-repair mechanisms and function as preventative medicine—or treatment if you're sick—it also relaxes your nervous system and helps heal your mind of depression, anxiety, fear, anger, and feelings of disconnection."

GAINING TRACTION AND MOVING FORWARD WITH SERVICE: SUE CLARK'S STORY

Every week during his tenure as president of BYU–Idaho, Elder Kim Clark and his wife, Sue, hosted open-forum question-and-answer sessions on campus for student family home evening groups. "One night," Sue related, "a sister stood up and said. 'I'm on medication for depression. Isn't it true that the Lord will take away my depression if I can just be good enough and prayerful enough and feel the Spirit enough?'"

Sue hadn't yet thought through whether she wanted anyone in her new community to know her depression story. "After all, I thought those students and the community needed me to be nearly perfect!" she says. "But because I could identify with the anguish I saw in the face of that sweet young sister, I said to her, 'I also suffer from depression, and so I will speak from my own personal experience.' What I told her, and what I tell students all the time now, is that when I am depressed I have a hard time feeling the Spirit, and I don't ever want to be without the Spirit. So I try to be diligent about doing what it takes for me not to let depression do that to me . . . because . . . I sometimes get to the point that I say to myself, 'I don't really have depression. I'm just a bad person. I need to be better.' But because I'm not feeling the Spirit, I have a hard time doing good and I begin to feel doomed."

Instead of surrendering to that feeling, Sue uses it as a cue to remind herself that she needs to seek encouragement from an outside source—a friend or her husband. It takes effort to do that, but more often than not it gives her precisely what she needs to get things moving in a positive direction, even if the moving is slow going and full of bursts and stops. After the fact, when the depression has waned, Sue says she can usually recognize that the intervention of a friend was actually an answer to her prayers, and although the Spirit felt absent, it was there all along as she shared her fears and discouragement with another.

Equally important—and very often necessary—is finding external support in a sympathetic medical doctor. Sometimes, in fact, when the Spirit seems the furthest away and hope is most dim, the greatest act of faith you can make is to seek out a psychiatrist or other physician who can work with you to find a medication best suited to your situation.

Sue says, "Every diagnosis of depression is individual, and the treatment for each person is tailored to [his or] her specific needs. Each of us has to figure it out. It took me a long time. From reading articles and papers on depression, I decided that I had enough symptoms that I probably needed a doctor to help me know what to do about it. Medication is only part of my treatment. I also know that how I manage my diet and exercise and sleep makes a huge difference."

Dr. Louise Jorgensen echoes this: "There's no question that a person who is depressed has their wheels on ice, and until they get traction they can't get off the ice. Sometimes the best way to get traction is through medication. In fact, a lot of times it's the only way to get traction."

I certainly found this to be true in my own treatment. What I also found particularly interesting, though, was what transpired once I began to seek medical intervention. The process of recovering and reclaiming mental well-being is strikingly parallel to the process of spiritual growth. Let me explain: Prayer is a powerful source of spiritual sustenance. It buoys us up, provides answers to questions, and is instrumental in fostering a relationship with our Savior. But it's not the only thing we can or must do to become spiritually strong. When we add scripture study, temple attendance, weekly repentance coupled with partaking of the sacrament, and a regimen of obedience and structure in our daily lives, that relationship with the Savior is strengthened. The same is true of treatment for depression. Medication provides the traction Dr. Jorgensen spoke of, but it is rarely enough on its own. To really break through and reopen the circuits that allow the Spirit to flow more freely and restore our reception, we need a regimen of complementary tools and behaviors.

Sue shared one of the tools that works particularly well for her. "Another huge thing I need to do," she says, "is make myself reach out to serve others. Service is actually one of the most important things I need to do.

"Service is not only a prime ingredient in the treatment of depression; it is a central part of the threads the Lord weaves into the fabric of our individual lives. When we are serving others we turn outward, away from ourselves, and to the Lord. It is such a blessing to be an instrument in His hands and feel His love for those we serve and His love for us. It is another paradox. He tells us to lose our lives to save our lives.

"I need to serve whenever I feel the least qualified to give of myself. In fact, that is when it is essential."

Sue shares an inspiring story of learning this lesson. During one period of depression when she was distraught and caught in a cycle of particularly negative self-talk, convinced she was failing at everything, especially motherhood, she knelt in prayer, pleading for some kind of breakthrough. During that prayer, she felt prompted to "serve someone else."

"I went back to bed that night," she says, "quite sure the thought had come from God because I would have never generated that idea in the frame of mind I was in, but I was also a little bit angry. How could that be the answer when I was already feeling overwhelmed?

"Well, He sent me on an errand. I ended up knocking on the door of a new sister in our ward one morning under the Lord's direction. When she answered the door she tearfully said, 'Thank you for coming. I had such a difficult night I thought I couldn't make it, but the Lord said, "Hang in there; Sue Clark will call in the morning."' I gathered . . . her family into our lives and under the canopy of the tapestry of our ward where everything they needed was accessed through professional people in our ward."

Reaching out to and serving someone else established a connection not just with a fellow sojourner on the path of righteousness but to the love of our Savior. For Sue, and many others, once they've reestablished some traction through medication or counseling, even the smallest act of service can increase the benefits of their treatment.

STRENGTH THROUGH REMEMBRANCE: THE TESTIMONY OF ANN MADSEN

I talked to Ann Madsen by phone one late fall afternoon, and she freely shared the details of a bout of depression she'd suffered that lasted almost nine months. More than four decades later, it's still vivid in her memory.

"Depression is very unique," she said. "There's a world of difference between depression and discouragement. After Truman [her husband] died, I was lonely and low and very unhappy, but I was not depressed. I was a free agent and could move away from the feelings. But when I was depressed, I couldn't move away. I couldn't get out of it. It was like I was in a sack and somebody had tied the top and I didn't know how to untie it. I couldn't get out."

At the time, Ann relates, "Only my husband knew and my bishop knew."

She spoke of her husband's kindness and compassion during her depression, but she herself felt like she was merely going through the motions of life. To be frank, she said, "I was faking it." Every day. Every task.

"I remember driving to my classes on campus and sitting down in class and thinking, 'If anyone knew how I feel right now they would be amazed.' It was like this hidden secret that I was carrying around with me.

"When you're in it, you feel very lonely; you think nobody else in the whole world would know how awful you feel and how bad your life has become.

"Every hour on the hour, I'd go into my bedroom in an empty house, kneel down, and say, 'I know you're there, God. I honestly believe you are there, but will you please do something for me? Help me out of this, I'm drowning.' For months, I felt that my prayer was hitting the ceiling. Sometimes I had a faint feeling, 'Yes, I'm here,' and that was it."

Ann was right on the edge of a nervous breakdown. There were days when she would say, "Dear Father, I just can't take one more day. I'm just going to give up." But she never did.

"It was the hardest thing I've ever been through in my life. I had medication. I had blessings. All I could do was the bare minimum of what was expected of me as a wife and mother."

Ann would plead with the Lord, "Heavenly Father, I just don't feel the Spirit now. Just let me feel the Spirit just a little bit." After months of praying, she finally had a breakthrough. She started to re-call times she *had* felt the Spirit in the past, especially on her mission with her husband.

"Every day [during our mission] there were miracles. I cannot deny the Spirit I felt then. So, I said to God, 'I have probably felt the Spirit more than any woman alive, and since that's the case, if I never feel it again, that's okay; I can rely on the way I felt then.' And it was amazing how these remembrances would come to my mind.

"That was a big turning point for me. It didn't cure my depression, but it changed my thought process."

Remembering is transformative. It's especially useful for depressed individuals who have become convinced they are worthless and estranged from the Spirit. I love how often the scriptures honor remembrance, commending its power as a spiritual tool.

Remembrance is one of the most pervasive themes of the Book of Mormon, and Moroni extolls it to the very end: "*Remember* how merciful the Lord hath been unto the children of men, from the creation of Adam even down until the time that ye shall receive these things, and ponder it in your hearts" (Moroni 10:3; emphasis added).

Moroni's concluding book also contains the sacrament prayers, which weekly renew our covenant with the Lord—and His with us—that if we will always *remember* Him, we will always have His Spirit with us (see Moroni 4; 5). We can exercise faith and hope in His promise, even when we are experiencing little spiritual light in the present moment. Our remembrance of Him and His remembrance of us are at the heart of our ongoing relationship, and it is not a relationship that He abandons.

Indeed, it is impossible for the Lord to forget us. Though we may sometimes feel that "The Lord hath forsaken me, and my Lord hath forgotten me," He responds with this harrowing, humbling image:

"Can a woman forget her sucking child, that she should not have compassion on the son of her womb? yea, they may forget, yet will I not forget thee.

"Behold, I have graven thee upon the palms of my hands" (Isaiah 49:14–16).

UPHELD BY AFFIRMATION: PATRESE

Patrese is a former stake Relief Society president, a wife, and a mother of four. When first diagnosed with bipolar disorder, she spent several nightmarish days in the hospital in isolation. She calls that experience her "personal Gethsemane."

"I'd never felt such intense pain. Anguish and terror overwhelmed me as I battled for control over my mind and body. My brain was just going haywire and I lost touch with reality. I felt abandoned and alone."

Despite her best efforts, her spiritual gauge was registering zero. No signals were penetrating, and she could not feel the presence of the Spirit—her mind was generating too much static.

Her husband, however, felt something entirely different the first time he was allowed to visit briefly during her hospital stay. When he walked into the room, he told her, he was overwhelmed by the Spirit; what it conveyed was love for Patrese. "That room became sacred to him because of what he felt, and that was Heavenly Father's love for me."

Although she couldn't feel anything but despair, her husband testified that the Spirit was indeed there, that Heavenly Father was still pouring down His love for her. It was tangible to him. This thought provided hope for Patrese as she worked to recover in the weeks and months that followed.

"The Spirit speaks to our minds and our hearts," she says. "If our minds are a garbled mess . . . we're not able to recognize that still, small voice. It just gets drowned out by the crisis that's happening."

Someone else's spoken testimony of God's love, or a priesthood blessing pronouncing His concern aloud, has been helpful to many who are experiencing despair at their inability to feel divine love. During a focus group I held in my home while researching this book, the benefit of spoken affirmations through priesthood blessings was mentioned over and over again, as you can see in the following conversation:

WOMAN #1: "There's a big difference between the Spirit not being present and me not being able to feel His presence. Sometimes, we don't distinguish that."

WOMAN #2: "For me, part of the key to managing my depression is having a set of people that in very dark times I trust to say, . . . 'I'm not feeling the Spirit so I need you to help me interpret it correctly and I'm going to choose to trust you because you're really all I've got.'"

WOMAN #3: "Yes, like when we're sitting in the same meeting and my husband just felt something very profound and I'm like, 'Huh, I got nothing.' That doesn't mean God is dead or absent, or that God is mad at me. I just couldn't feel it right then and that might not be my fault."

WOMAN #4: "This is how I got my testimony of priesthood blessings . . . because there are times that you cannot feel the Spirit of God, so you need to hear it from someone else's voice. I've learned I need to ask for blessings. I've also found with close friends, when I recognize that they're depressed, sometimes I'll say to them, 'Would you mind if my husband gave you a blessing? Because I think there are things that you need to hear that you can't feel right now.'"

WOMAN #2: "Yes, because sometimes you cannot feel anything positive, you cannot feel anything spiritual, but that auditory experience can at least remind you that God loves you, that you're not alone, and sometimes that creates images for you, like the Lord is watching over you. Things you can't feel, but then you can see or hear."

WOMAN #1: "I do think that's part of a beautiful thing that we've got going here as a community of Saints."

It really is beautiful! And the doctrine in it is also astounding: our suffering, or weakness, may not be taken away, but the Lord can use it to make us strong and to help us endure. Knowing, through words spoken aloud, that we are loved of God strengthens our will. Paul teaches this lesson well. In 2 Corinthians 12:7, he wrote of his own despair, his "thorn in the flesh." We don't know what that thorn was, but we do know that Paul asked the Lord three times to remove it before he received an answer—a long-sought-after answer that did not involve taking away the thorn. Instead it offered comfort. The Savior's promise to sustain Paul in his struggles—and Paul's testimony—was this:

"And he said unto me, My grace is sufficient for thee: for my strength is made perfect in weakness. Most gladly therefore will I rather glory in my infirmities, that the power of Christ may rest upon me.

"Therefore I take pleasure in infirmities, in reproaches, in necessities, in persecutions, in distresses for Christ's sake: for when I am weak, then am I strong" (2 Corinthians 12:9–10).

RECLAIMING A BRIGHTNESS OF HOPE

For most people who are diagnosed with depression, it isn't a single event. The disease comes and goes throughout their lives, differing in intensity and duration. Like Paul's "thorn in the flesh," it is never removed completely. Most of those I interviewed, however, reported that the numbness and heartache associated with the perceived absence of the Spirit was easier to bear in those second, third, and fourth wrestles with their illness. Because their access to the Spirit had once resumed, they believed it would return again. They also took advantage of the strategies they found helpful the first time to combat their depression. For some, like Robert Millet, sharing their story is therapeutic; for others, like Sue Clark, service propels their momentum towards recovery once traction has been restored by medication or therapy. Still others, like Ann Madsen, find that actively seeking memories of past spiritual experiences can substitute during the dearth of current ones. For Patrese, receiving affirmation that she is loved and valued is crucial; there are many for whom this is strengthening. Many scriptures reassure us on this point as well: God does not abandon us. "Whither shall I go from thy spirit? or whither shall I flee from thy presence? If I ascend up into heaven, thou art there: if I make my bed in hell, behold, thou art there. If I take the wings of the morning, and dwell in the uttermost parts of the sea; even there shall thy hand lead me, and thy right hand shall hold me" (Psalm 139:7–10). Often, it is a combination of these spiritual supports that will provide help and restore hope.

CHAPTER 3

THE STORM CLOUD OF STIGMA

They looked unto him, and were lightened:
and their faces were not ashamed.

—PSALM 34:5

As a student at Brigham Young University some thirty years ago, Laurie decided to finally pay a visit to the campus health center. No matter how much she slept, she told the doctor—and there were days that she couldn't get out of bed at all—she felt exhausted. She had trouble concentrating, was unaccountably irritable and short-tempered, and, most alarmingly, had been experiencing chest pains, shortness of breath, hot flashes, and other symptoms of panic. Laurie thought she had a virus, but to her deep embarrassment and dismay, the doctor diagnosed her with depression and anxiety, gave her a bottle of pills and a prescription for a refill, and sent her on her way. The minute she got back to her apartment, she flushed the pills down the toilet.

In the years that followed, Laurie graduated from BYU, met and married her husband, and gave birth to two children. Through it all, she never told anyone about her diagnosis—or the symptoms she continued to experience. She hid them in shame, rejoicing during the periods of normalcy that came when they ebbed, and suffering in silence when they roared back like a raging river. Finally, after her third child was born, she talked to a doctor again—and this time, she took the medication that he prescribed. She was amazed a few weeks later: she started to feel better! She marveled that she'd gone so long without seeking help. What had she been thinking!

Laurie's story is not uncommon. "I felt like I shouldn't need medication," she recalls. "I was convinced I should be able to pick myself up by the bootstraps and do it myself." The handful of people that Laurie had known who were willing to take medication were all family members, and she had, even if somewhat subconsciously, relegated them to the "crazy category." Would people think that *she* was crazy if they found out what the doctor had told her? Would they think God was punishing her for some reason? What if she *was* crazy?

Though a huge cloud of stigma still surrounds depression and mental illness, Laurie has joined the growing movement to dispel it. Once she realized how much better she could feel, she thought, "What's crazy is how afraid of this we all are!" From that point on, she says, "I have talked about depression and mental illness and done my best to let everyone know—'Look at me! I have depression. And I'm normal!'" Laurie has made it her mission to reach out to others who are suffering under the double burden of mental illness and stigma. More and more often, they are reaching out to her.

Stigma is attached to the medications and other therapies that provide depression sufferers with relief as much as it is to mental illness itself. "The Lord provides ways for us to overcome all of the obstacles that we have in this earthly existence," Laurie says, "but it's not always the way we think it's going to be. A lot of times, it's through scientific discovery. I've learned that we need to be open-minded, and not only to medicine but to all of the scientific discoveries that are being made about how the brain and the body work and why certain things happen to us."

THE COMPLICATION OF SHAME

An estimated 350 million people worldwide experience an episode of clinical depression each year. Fewer than half of them seek help. Some are living in places where mental-health resources are scarce; many can't afford to pay for treatment even if it is available. But a significant number, especially in the developed world, are scared away by the stigma associated with depression. Others who do seek help do so quietly, confiding only in their therapist or doctor about "their secret," severing connections to other sources of support. "The experience of social rejection and isolation that comes from stigma has the potential for direct harmful effects," *Psychology Today* reported in 2014. Moreover, "people with mental health issues . . . internalize this stigma to develop a strong 'self-stigma.' This self-stigma will often undermine self-efficacy, resulting in a 'why try' attitude that can worsen prospects of recovery."

These tendencies are even more marked in the Latter-day Saint community. Virtually every one of the men and women I interviewed for this book reported issues with stigma. Their confessions are heartbreaking but revealing:

LEO: "Depression is something that we don't talk about very much and that we sort of sweep under the rug. . . . Those who struggle with it tend to hide as much as we can, because there is a feeling of shame or guilt, or even feeling broken, like you don't want people to know that you're broken."

MARIN: "Those interactions I had with other people who said, you know, 'Go to the temple or just serve more, or are you praying enough?' It made me feel like this was something that wasn't real. And I felt like I have a problem that I can't fix, and that no one believes is real. And it . . . it was just so shameful. If you tell someone, 'Oh, I have heart disease,' or, 'I have a broken leg,' they're so helpful. Can we bring you meals, how can we help you? Can we do this? What can we do? If you tell people you have depression, they look at you like you're crazy."

HEIDI: "I wish I wasn't so prideful about it, and that it didn't have such a stigma. This is sure a time when both of us could use some support. But we don't want people to think we are crazy, so we carry heavy burdens in silence."

SYDNEY: "This is where a lot of this stigma comes from; it's right in our own homes. We don't even need to talk about it outside with our friends to feel bad.

"I remember when I first started to see a therapist . . . one of my parents was like, 'So, when is your next appointment with that person?' I'm like, 'The therapist? He's a therapist. I'm going to see a therapist.'

"She said, 'Oh.'

"Right there in our mostly loving and open relationships we have a stigma as we're trying to figure out what's going on in our minds."

JEN: "I think we need to talk about it as 'brain health' instead of 'mental health.' Think of the brain as an organ, as a part of your body instead of a capacity of your body. . . . Our pediatrician reminds me that people talk about the brain all the time. We also talk about heart health, and blood health. If we rephrase it and talk about 'brain health,' it might change some of the stigma."

CELIA: "When this all started happening [with my daughter's depression], it was so surreal. I felt like it was someone else's life. I felt like a failure as a mom, like I had done something wrong. Also, culturally, it's not something that people talk about. You don't call your best friend or neighbor and ask them for a good therapist, like you would a chicken pot pie recipe."

ROBERT: "What really scares me is not allowing our kids to know that we adults have struggles with this. . . . What's it say to our kids or the youth if they think that we're hiding it or we don't want to talk about it?

"The kids will mimic what we do. We're their examples. If they think that we are either ashamed of this illness or that it's something to be kept secret, then they're going to think the same thing and how are they going to get the help they need? They may think, 'My parents are going to be ashamed of me. They're ashamed of the illness in themselves. They're going to be ashamed of the illness in me.' I just think we need to be more open about it."

OLLIE: "My mother came to me and just said, 'Snap out of it.' It's not about putting my mother down, she was the best mother anyone could have ever had; she was just concerned and so were others that said that. It was not out of bad intent; they just hadn't experienced it and didn't understand it. I would have given all four limbs and anything else I could; I would have given anything to snap out of it. I just had no ability to do that.

"That was probably the most painful thing anyone could say, was to snap out of it, because I did not have the ability to do it."

A TALE OF TWO SISTERS

One woman offers the poignant example of her two sisters to illustrate the devastating effects of the stigma and shame associated with depression. The first sister has struggled with mental illness throughout her life and was recently hospitalized again for major depression. The second sister had just been diagnosed with stage-four cancer. The reactions of others to each sister were vastly different.

For the sister with cancer, "there's been an outpouring of love and kindness and support and 'what can we do for you,' and donations to a fund to help pay for expenses and all of the things that are going to come up. People have donated thousands of dollars to this fund. . . . People are [calling] and saying, 'We're so sorry and we feel so terrible about what's happened to you. We'll do anything we can to try to support you and love you through this,' which she deserves. She richly deserves this. It's just an awful situation."

For her sister with depression, however, there has been nothing anywhere close to this type of reaction. "There's not an outpouring of love. There's not Facebook notes and emails and letters and cards coming in in the same way. It's just, 'Oh, there she goes again. She's back in the hospital.' Even from people who love her, there's frustration and judgment that my sister with cancer does not have."

In fact, the sister with depression confided, "I so wish I could be in [the sister with cancer]'s shoes. I would take the death that is coming her way. It would be such a relief for me to be able to die in a nonembarrassing way. I would just love to have my own troubles come to an end and have it be in a way that people wouldn't judge me and could reach out to my kids and be kind and loving to them and take care of them."

Depression affects every facet of a sufferer's life, even—and perhaps most grievously—the religious aspect. If simply getting out of bed and taking a shower is difficult, leaving the house and going out among strangers can appear mind-bendingly impossible, as can dragging oneself to church every Sunday to be inspected by people who know you and may be all too inclined to judge you.

One woman confides that she's lived with depression nearly all of her adult life. With time, and lots of experience, she's learned how to manage it, how to force herself to get up and go, even when another episode strikes and she's not yet found treatment that works. At those times, she wrote me in an email, going to church is almost impossible:

"In my darkest times, I have not felt like going to church. It's not that I don't believe it's true, but rather (1) I'm not comfortable going somewhere where everyone is happy and friendly when I am feeling horrible about myself or my life; (2) I can't imagine feeling the way everyone else is acting, so it feels to me like they are all hypocrites; (3) I'm afraid if someone asks how I'm doing, I will just begin to cry; and (4) When I am in a depressed state, many of the things taught in church just feel like condemnation to me, reinforcing my already negative beliefs about myself. . . . It makes me wonder how many semi-inactives out there are in the same situation but don't really realize why they struggle with attending church."

How many *are* absent from the pews in sacrament meeting because of stigma—external or internally imposed, real or imagined? How many could we reach if we regarded depression as the illness it is and not as a spiritual malady, and if we really talked about it, openly and in church? What if we offered unconditional support and love to one another instead of judgment and advice to just "pray more" or simply "snap out of it"?

The most common manifestations of external stigma reported to me were the perspective that depression isn't a real disease, the belief that a sufferer might be dangerous and/or incapable of fulfilling duties in a job or a Church calling, and the impression that someone with depression is simply too weak to take control of his or her condition. The frequently reported elements of self-stigma were feelings of guilt, shame, and embarrassment; a reluctance to share the diagnosis with others; and a broad, insidious desire to distance oneself from others socially.

Remarkably, a number of the men and women I spoke with have been able to let go of the self-stigma. Even more are hopeful that the external elements of stigma can be overcome as medical science makes advances in treatment and as more individuals like Laurie willingly share their stories. By speaking openly and honestly, Laurie says, she feels depression becomes more normalized, and others can talk to her about it as if they were talking about any other medical condition. "I always say that I'm the happiest depressed person you'll ever meet because my life is just full of joy and happiness," she says. "But I do things on a regular basis to make sure that I don't struggle. I take my medicine. I get exercise. I try to get enough sleep. I try to eat right. I treat my depression as if it's a chronic illness, *which of course it is.*"

The misconceptions she held when she was first diagnosed at BYU are gone. Instead of thinking depression is a weakness within her, she sees it as an earthly struggle she has been asked to face. "It's just as if you have diabetes or something that you have to pay attention to every day," she says, adding that you have to treat it and monitor it and take care of yourself, and part of that self-care is sharing your experience with others. "It's very easy for me now to say, 'Well, this is my experience. This might be helpful to you. I'm not perfect, and yet I am still capable of serving. I've been Relief Society president for nine years. I was stake Young Women president for seven years. I am still righteous, even though I will have this struggle with me my whole life.'"

One facet of stigma many work hard to overcome is the notion that depression is a symptom of spiritual weakness. In fact, the opposite is often true. As with other adversities, learning to understand and deal with depression can and does help us grow spiritually. I love how Kalli, an artist, described it to me:

"I felt like an Etch-A-Sketch. I created this beautiful picture on my Etch-A-Sketch of who I was. Somehow it got shaken. That picture got erased. I was down to nothing. I think that's how God actually works. These experiences seem so terrifying, so horrendous when you're depressed.

"For a long time it is a mess. We also have to learn to be okay with the mess. Life's messy, and it's okay. We are messy, and it's okay."

Educating others about depression and helping them understand that it's not the result of weakness or sin is one of the best first steps that members of The Church of Jesus Christ of Latter-day Saints can take to fight the stigma surrounding the disease. In doing so, we imitate Jesus, who modeled this behavior with the blind man as recorded in John, chapter 9. His own disciples misunderstood the man's condition as a punishment, asking Jesus, "Master, who did sin, this man, or his parents, that he was born blind?" The Master responded with love, a lesson, and a miracle: "Neither hath this man sinned, nor his parents: but that the works of God should be made manifest in him." Jesus personally anointed the man's eyes with clay and instructed him to wash in the pool of Siloam. The man went and did as the Savior told him to and was healed (John 9:1–7).

When those who are depressed lose their fear of being blamed for their condition, opportunities for both love and miracles are created. Healing may not come right away or in a literal fashion, but when stigma is lifted, so too is the heavy burden of shame.

HELPING OTHERS UNDERSTAND:
ROBERT'S STORY

In his ward in the heart of Texas, Robert is a disciple who strives to lighten burdens by challenging the stigma associated with depression. He retired from the United States Army as a medical doctor and now is a university lecturer. He has moved his wife and children many times, including overseas. Despite his prestigious job and a beautiful, loving family, major depression still afflicts him for long periods at a time. Robert explains that in addition to the physical pain depression causes, the intense spiritual and psychic distress is a great trial of his faith. He often asks himself, "'Hey, Robert, do you really have faith? Are you going to remain true?' These are questions that come to me in these episodes that really have, I think, challenged my faith as to whether I'm 100 percent committed to my Savior."

Even in the midst of his own battle, Robert never stops talking about that battle with others, helping them understand what depression is and how it works. Maybe it's the doctor in him, but he feels driven to help others who are suffering. "What I tell people," he says, "is that this is an illness just like any other illness. You can say all the prayers you want and you can live completely righteously, but it doesn't necessarily mean that you're going to be healed of an illness. You might be. You might receive a blessing that would cure you. I firmly believe you need to use the priesthood and medical care in dealing with depression. But depression is a trial, and some of us simply have to endure this one."

Robert and his wife, Michele, have put together a presentation they give in various meetings to educate others about depression. They explain what depression is, discussing how it strikes arbitrarily and hits individuals with symptoms that vary from despondency to indifference to anger and extreme emotional pain. They discuss treatment options. They also talk about how to engage those who are in its throes and love and accept them as they are. Robert is always surprised by the number of people who approach him afterward and say, "You just described exactly what I'm feeling."

He wants people to know that no matter how bad they're feeling, depression doesn't have to mean that "life's going to be a mess, or you're never going to accomplish anything." He says, "If I look at my life professionally, let alone my experience in church, I see that I have a beautiful family. I've got wonderful friends. Professionally I've done so much. It's important to know that you can have depression and still become a doctor. You can still do great science. You can still have a family and serve and bless others. I think that's an important message to get out there."

"WHERE CAN I TURN FOR PEACE?"
THE WOMEN BEHIND THE HYMN

Robert's message highlights another step in combatting the stigma of depression: persuading others that depression is a disease, not an identity. A diagnosis of depression does not mean that life is over or that there will never be joy again.

A wise therapist once told me that life isn't really about being happy. It's about finding peace. This lesson struck me with renewed force when I learned the story behind our beloved Latter-day Saint hymn "Where Can I Turn for Peace?" (*Hymns*, no. 129)

Where can I turn for peace?
Where is my solace
When other sources cease to make me whole?
When with a wounded heart, anger, or malice,
I draw myself apart,
Searching my soul?

***

Where, when my aching grows,
Where, when I languish,
Where, in my need to know, where can I run?
Where is the quiet hand to calm my anguish?
Who, who can understand?
He, only One.

***

He answers privately,
Reaches my reaching
In my Gethsemane, Savior and Friend.
Gentle the peace he finds for my beseeching.
Constant he is and kind,
Love without end.

The lyricist, the late Emma Lou Warner Thayne, was brilliant. A devoted wife, a mother of five daughters, a champion tennis player, and a professor at the University of Utah for more than thirty years, she inspired men and women the world over with her writings. She wrote honestly and served admirably in many callings in the Church. And she struggled mightily to find peace amid severe trials that threatened her family, including her oldest daughter's battle with mental illness. For three years, Emma Lou did everything she could to solve the mystery of her daughter's suffering, to find peace and help for a diagnosis she knew little about. She called it "the bleakest time I had ever known."

In the midst of this adversity, she was asked by the Church to compose a song for the finale of an annual conference of the Mutual Improvement Association, the organization for young men and women at the time. Initially, Emma Lou doubted she could find the words for a song that would unite and inspire the youth. Nevertheless, she resorted to a quiet room in her basement and began the process. She later wrote about it in the *Church News:*

"Sitting at my makeshift desk I asked on paper what I had implored—so many times. 'Where can I turn for peace? Where is my solace? When with a wounded heart, anger, or malice, I draw myself apart, searching my soul?' Three verses of a poem found their way to the page, voicing my anguish and providing the answer I carried in my heart. 'He answers privately, reaches my reaching in my Gethsemane, Savior and Friend.'

"I called Joleen [who composed the music for the hymn]. She had a history of genetic depression in her family, so she understood every word I'd written. She sat at her piano, and as I read a line, she composed a line. By noon we had our hymn."

I was so inspired by Emma Lou's story, I knew I wanted to speak with Joleen Meredith myself. Joleen told me that she and Emma Lou had called their song the "Mental-Health Hymn" and that the

Gethsemane they were both thinking of as they wrote it included the mental suffering and anguish that the Savior took upon Himself for each individual who has or will suffer from depression and other mental illnesses. She then told me about a "mental-health episode" of her own. It was so severe, she recalled, that she was unable to get out of bed for months. When she was finally able to leave her room and go downstairs, she joked that she and her family "celebrated by getting in the car and driving around the block." After the episode eased and Joleen found help, she became a lobbyist for mental-health issues and served on the Utah Governor's Board of Mental Health and Substance Abuse. Her goal, she said, was to erase the stigma attached to mental illness and encourage people to look for help.

I loved visiting with Joleen because she made it easy to talk about mental illness. She spoke with candor and even a little bit of humor. She wishes that mental-health issues were as easy to spot as physical issues. "Too bad you can't wear a cast on your head," she laughed, "because something is broken in here, and that's really hard for people to understand."

Then and now, Joleen believes that peace *can* be found, even when trapped in the Gethsemane of depression—even when the Lord does not heal us like He did the blind man. Prayer can definitely help. But healing can come so much faster, she says, when we permit ourselves to use all the tools God has given us to fight this illness. "If something were wrong with your ear, you wouldn't go to a foot doctor," she says. "If something is broken in your mind, go to the right doctor *and* go to God."

NOT STANDING DOWN: THE WITNESS OF STEPHEN ROBINSON

Just as Emma Lou Thayne and Joleen Meredith's landmark hymn has brought peace to many a listener, the late Stephen E.

Robinson's immensely popular "Parable of the Bicycle" has brought a greater understanding of grace to countless readers. Stephen was a longtime professor at Brigham Young University, chair of the Department of Ancient Scripture, and a bishop. He was also a fearless stigma breaker.

Stephen frankly shared his depression story with me—as he did with anyone who asked. "When I was fifty-two years old," he said, "I hit a brick wall, and I had a depressive episode so serious I was suicidal. We locked the gun cabinets. They kept saying, 'Give us two weeks and we'll have you properly medicated.' Three years later, I was still just hanging on by my fingernails. It took three to five years for that depression to lift . . . but the upside was that I knew what was happening."

Stephen had experienced depression in the past; he'd become accustomed to slogging through it while he and his doctors worked to find the right treatment. He knew from experience that its onset was not tied to any specific thing that he was doing and that it eventually lifted. When he finally returned to teaching full time, a number of his colleagues encouraged him to keep quiet about his ordeal. He refused. Instead, he stood up in front of his students and talked about his long journey through the dark night of depression.

The result? Students lined up by the dozens to talk to him after his classes.

I asked him what these students wanted to know.

"They wanted to know why they were in hell emotionally," he responded. "Why they couldn't feel the Spirit and what could they do about it. I personally took fifty students either to the BYU Counseling Center or to a couple of counselors I knew here in Provo and got them help."

Almost all of the students told him that they'd tried to share their problems with their parents or their bishop or someone else that they respected, but had been told again and again to pray harder, study the scriptures more deeply, and repent more sincerely. Like the disciples with the blind man, the people they'd turned to for help couldn't have been less helpful if they'd tried. Depression is a disease, not a spiritual deficit.

In the years since Stephen helped the students who lined up at his office door to recognize depression as the disease that it is, the Church has likewise made tremendous strides in delivering that message. Elder Jeffrey R. Holland's October 2013 general conference talk was followed by the release of a website designed specifically to support those who deal with mental illnesses. The site's message is one of hope and authenticity; it doesn't skirt around the topic or romanticize mental illness but provides real resources to help, including true—often heartbreaking—stories from other Latter-day Saints who suffer, as well as links to suicide hotlines and therapy possibilities.

ERIN, EMPATHY, AND PLASTIC BRACELET AWARENESS

In the grip of a depressive episode, it's hard to feel anything but discouraged. But once medication takes effect, and therapy allows light to seep back in, something good almost always happens. When the cloud dissipated for Erin, she found herself with vastly increased empathy and a burning desire to help others. My initial intent was to learn about her struggles with depression in her childhood and adolescence. Though she did share that part of her story with me, it was what she did during her *healthy* periods that turned out to be the bigger story.

Several years ago, Erin learned that the daughter of a good friend was in the hospital for depression and suicidal ideation. It got her thinking about what often happens when ward members learn that a fellow Saint is hospitalized with other illnesses—appendicitis, pneumonia, heart problems, and so on. The room overflows with cards and flowers. A steady stream of visitors stops by to say hello. At home, the family is brought hot meals and offers of service. But from bitter experience, Erin knew how lonely it is to be hospitalized with depression. Sometimes this is because the patient keeps the condition a secret, but often it's because others are afraid—they don't know what to say or how to react, and therefore they stay away.

Erin decided to change this. "After the first week, I went to see her," she told me. "I bought a little bouquet and a goody and some slippers. And I told her that I was surprised and angry with myself that it took me so long to come. I knew when she went in—I knew the first moment she went in—because I'm good friends with her mother, so I knew that whole week. I was being supportive to her mother, and talking to her, but not to the girl in the hospital. I said, 'I'm sorry that it took me so long to realize that. . . . I want you to know that I know you're here, and I know how hard it is, and I know you're on life support, and if it were any other kind of life support for any other condition, you'd have a hundred people calling and sending cards, and your friends, and ward members, and roommates, and everybody else would be here to see you.'"

Erin went home that day wondering what more she could do. She started thinking about all the pink paraphernalia and bracelets and other things that people wear to show their support for women with breast cancer and how wonderful that was. And then she went to work creating an emblem of her own, a metaphor for this moment. Erin took a clear plastic water bottle and cut a ring right out of the middle of it. It was just the right size for a bracelet, simple, but pretty. And as depression often is—and as depressed people too often feel they are—it was also almost invisible.

The next day Erin brought the bracelet to her young friend and gave several more to her friend's family and to the staff at the hospital.

"I told her, 'Unfortunately, your condition is kind of invisible; people don't want to see it. They don't want to know about it. . . . But we're all here, wearing a bracelet to support you.'"

Erin remembers her own first experiences with depression—how harrowing they were, and how isolated they made her feel. "Depression is just like a dirty trick on one's life," she says. "Here you are, living your life, thinking, okay, this is great, and then, wham. You've got to deal with this thing. You don't know what it is. You don't understand it, and it doesn't make any sense."

When we say "I understand" or "I care" during bedside visits, or when we wear a nearly invisible bracelet in support, we can encourage others to seek help or to feel safe enough to express their experiences and feelings. Our acknowledgment will validate depression as an illness like any other, shattering the external and internal stigma. I envision a day, coming soon, when we will visit at the bedsides of those in mental-health facilities as easily as in the cancer wing of the hospital. And we can carry with us into the spiritually dark realm of depression a testimony that there is no judgment and no cause for shame. The Lord's love encompasses this ailment, and so does ours.

It's a little thing, as small as a mustard seed, but like the scriptures say about faith, it can move mountains.

CHAPTER 4

Toxic Perfectionism

Come unto Christ, and be perfected in him.

—Moroni 10:32

S everal years before I was diagnosed with major depressive disorder, I published my first book on a topic about which I feel passionate: being a mother. That book rejected the notion that a woman who chooses motherhood is "just a mom." There is much more to motherhood than this belittling phrase implies! My book championed mothers and the sacrifices they make. I related stories that encourage women to take care of themselves, pursue their other interests when possible, and remember that—just like their own children— they are beloved daughters of God. I shared anecdotes and life lessons learned, including one that had become my mantra in the days when I was single and working full time in New York City on the CBS *Early Show:* Don't let the praise define you or the criticism will kill you.

Then, even though I believed every word I wrote in that book, I found myself several years later slowly killing myself with criticism. Over time I'd become convinced I wasn't good enough: not a good enough mother, not a good enough wife, not a good enough friend, not good enough at anything.

These days, I sometimes refer to myself as a recovering perfectionist. On that bleak day when I asked a friend if she'd be willing to care for my children if I weren't around, however, I had no idea how dangerous perfectionism can be, especially in combination with depression and suicidal ideation.

A paper published by the American Psychological Association in 2014 reports that the link between perfectionism and suicide is stronger than previously believed and distressingly underrecognized. The reasons vary, but a big part of it is the "not-good-enough" cycle. A perfectionist who is depressed and caught in a cycle of negative rumination often also feels that he or she is living an inauthentic life. This stems from the desire to hide every flaw and present a put-together, successful exterior while battling a convincing inner voice insinuating that one is failing at every turn. "The feeling," according to the paper's authors, "of living an inauthentic life contributes to a negative self-view and sense of despair and imposterism while also reminding the self-presenter on a continuing basis that he or she is far from perfect." Because people in this situation tend to self-present well, despite depression and even suicidal ideation, friends and family members often don't recognize that they're in jeopardy and vulnerable to the traps depression constantly sets in the mind. A woman referenced in the paper had no idea what her husband was contemplating before he took his own life. Now, she warns, "I have been learning that perfectionism plus depression is a loaded gun."

As a member of The Church of Jesus Christ of Latter-day Saints, I worry that the Saints are at an even greater risk than many regarding the "loaded gun" of perfectionism. These fears are echoed by experts in the field; Dr. Kris Doty-Yells is one of them. Several years ago, as a crisis worker in the emergency room at Utah Valley Regional Medical Center, she started noticing an interesting phenomenon on Sunday afternoons. "We would get people that would come in, women mostly, starting at about 12:15 on Sunday afternoons. . . . They were experiencing acute anxiety and depression, but what brought them in was typically one of two things. One was that they would have heard a talk in church or a lesson that would have instilled some guilt and shame in them, and the other one was that they might have received a Church calling and suddenly be feeling completely inadequate." Their responses were increased displays of depressive symptoms and tangible, physical panic attacks.

Dr. Doty-Yells didn't draw conclusions but decided to investigate the phenomenon after she was hired at Utah Valley University as department chair and associate professor of social work. She began a qualitative exploratory study to identify what puts women who are members of the Church at risk for depression. The study included interviews with active Latter-day Saint women who had been clinically diagnosed with major depression. The results identified five specific risk factors: genetics, a history of abuse, family relationships, feeling judged by others, and toxic perfectionism.

The last one was a bit surprising. Being a perfectionist is often seen as a desirable trait. Employers, for example, favor perfectionists because they're attentive to details and have high standards at work. Teachers love perfectionists, who tend to complete homework and submit it on time. But for the perfectionist who is also clinically depressed or dealing with another mental illness, such as generalized anxiety disorder or anorexia nervosa, these self-imposed high standards can become a nightmare. A depressed teenager, for example, might not turn in her homework at all because she's paralyzed by the fear that it's not perfect. Instead of a best effort, there's no effort—because it won't be perfect. A few rounds of this type of thinking and she's failing the class, increasingly depressed, subject to ongoing negative rumination, and, as more and more studies demonstrate, at increasing risk of suicide.

Add a religious culture that sometimes misconstrues the Savior's admonition to "Be ye therefore perfect, even as your Father which is in heaven is perfect" (Matthew 5:48), and a real tempest can begin to brew. When he was president of Brigham Young University, Elder Cecil O. Samuelson addressed students there about the dangers of this storm.

"It will be an even better year for each of us personally if we can avoid making unnecessary or foolish personal mistakes," Elder Samuelson said as the school year opened. "You may believe I am talking only about slothfulness or Honor Code violations. *Equally concerning to me is the rather common problem of perfectionism.*

"One area of confusion not rare among us is the notion that worthiness is synonymous with perfection. It is not! One can be fully worthy in a gospel sense and yet still be growing while dealing with personal imperfections. It might be understandable to believe . . . perfectionism is laudable. In fact it is not. It is corrosive and destructive and is the antithesis of the healthy quest for eventual perfection that the Savior prescribes."

More recently, Elder Jeffrey R. Holland addressed the topic in general conference:

"What I now say in no way denies or diminishes any commandment God has ever given us. I believe in His perfection, and I know we are His spiritual sons and daughters with divine potential to become as He is. I also know that as children of God *we should not demean or vilify ourselves,* as if beating up on ourselves is somehow going to make us the person God wants us to become. No! With a willingness to repent and a desire for increased righteousness always in our hearts, *I would hope we can pursue personal improvement in a way that doesn't include getting ulcers or anorexia, feeling depressed or demolishing self-esteem. That is not what the Lord wants.*" Indeed, the Lord surely wouldn't give us a commandment that we could fulfill only while also damaging our health and "demolishing" our self-esteem, Elder Holland explained.

Seeing the commandment to "be ye therefore perfect" that way is what Dr. Doty-Yells calls putting Matthew 5:48 "on steroids." Some members, more often women than men, she says, see the word *perfect* in there and think, "Okay, I've got to be perfect. I have to be without flaw. I have to be without mistake. I have to appear to be this way because it's absolutely impossible for me to actually be like that, so since I can't be perfect I can at least give the illusion that [I am], and so in order to do that, I have to elevate myself above everyone else."

Usually, the process isn't so blatant, she explains. The depressed individual comes to this conclusion almost subconsciously. What isn't subconscious, however, is the sudden realization that he or she is being inauthentic. The cycle begins again.

I used to find myself caught in this cycle. For years, I was very careful not to let anyone into my house unless it was perfectly clean. I was so particular about this that if we had people over for dinner, I would have Mark carry piles of our stuff upstairs and stack it in a bedroom so the family room, kitchen, and all the living spaces looked perfectly spotless. After guests left, we'd bring everything back downstairs to "live again." I had convinced myself that a clean house was a reflection of me as a person—of my mothering skills, of my homemaking skills, of my time-management skills, and so on. Oh, the anxiety it created!

Pair this tendency with depression—I already believed I wasn't good enough—and you can image how extreme the negative self-talk became. The isolation was worse. When we'd cart the stacks of stuff back downstairs to resume our normal, not-so-orderly lives, I would feel a bit ashamed, worrying what others would think if they discovered I was faking it. On one occasion when a woman from the ward was over for some reason, she looked around and with a little envy, maybe even a tinge of hostility, said, "Everything is so *clean.*" If she only knew! I think I did say, jokingly, that all the messes had been transported upstairs. I should have physically walked her upstairs and shown her the piles of stuff stacked on the bed and on the floor of our bedroom.

Not long ago, one of our children participated in an art therapy program that combined counseling with creative expression as a technique to deal with anxiety. It was, frankly, an education for me as much as it was for my child. It really helped both of us. On this particular day, a fresh-faced, young arts specialist showed up to run the class. I don't think she had any idea how powerful and memorable her little project would be.

She rolled out a crate stacked with boxes, most of them about the size of a shoe box. On a separate cart, she presented us with a huge stack of magazines, scissors, and tape. Our assignment was to pick out a box and work together to create a piece of art she called our "Authenticity Box." On the outside of the box, we were instructed to tape all sorts of pictures that represented who we are—pictures we cut out of how we present ourselves to other people and how we want others to view us. This was our "image." On the inside of the box, we were to tape pictures that depict who we really are—behind closed doors when no one else is around.

We got to work. It took us about an hour. At the end came the lesson: the more similar the outside and inside of your box, the healthier your mental state. It was a wakeup call, an immediate, visual reminder of everything that is wrong with perfectionism, with requiring ourselves to meet an impossible standard championed by an outside force. When trying to live up to this standard, we are prone to pride, defeatism, debilitating comparisons, and a picture of ourselves as something we might not actually be. We are inauthentic. While focusing on the Savior's plan for perfection, however, we work on what is inside. We don't worry so much about the outside. We abandon pride, stop comparing ourselves to others, and don't try to go it alone—we allow the Savior to save us.

THE PSALM OF NEPHI

The great prophet Nephi (I wonder if *he* was a bit of a perfectionist and experienced his own periods of at least situational depression) lamented his sins and feared that they had destroyed his peace and afflicted his soul:

"If I have seen so great things," he writes in the beautiful psalm he composed after his father's death, "if the Lord in his condescension unto the children of men hath visited men in so much mercy, why should my heart weep and my soul linger in the valley of sorrow, and my flesh waste away, and my strength slacken, because of mine afflictions?" (2 Nephi 4:26).

Boy, is that a familiar question! Fortunately, Nephi didn't just ask it. In the midst of his darkest moment, he also provided the answer: that he remembered the many times past when his heart had soared because of divine help. He reminded himself to rejoice and continue to trust in the Lord; it is He, rather than we, who supplies the missing perfecting pieces:

"Notwithstanding the great goodness of the Lord, in showing me his great and marvelous works, my heart exclaimeth: O wretched man that I am! Yea, my heart sorroweth because of my flesh; my soul grieveth because of mine iniquities.

"I am encompassed about, because of the temptations and the sins which do so easily beset me.

"And when I desire to rejoice, my heart groaneth because of my sins; *nevertheless, I know in whom I have trusted.*

"My God hath been my support; he hath led me through mine afflictions in the wilderness; and he hath preserved me upon the waters of the great deep.

"He hath filled me with his love, even unto the consuming of my flesh. . . .

"Awake, my soul! No longer droop in sin. Rejoice, O my heart, and give place no more for the enemy of my soul. . . .

"O Lord, I have trusted in thee, and I will trust in thee forever" (2 Nephi 4:17–21, 28, 34; emphasis added).

There is immense hope in this passage. If Nephi could be brought so low despite his great works and spiritual prowess, those who roam through the fog of depression are not alone. Elder Holland offers this profound thought: "If sometimes the harder you try, the harder it gets, take heart. So it has been with the best people who ever lived."

"COULD ANYTHING MAKE ME FEEL DIFFERENTLY": JILL'S STORY

Many women mentioned the appearance of their homes or their children, the way they taught lessons in church, how they looked, and what others thought of them as they shared their stories of depression with me. The desire to be "good enough" is debilitating for the depressed or anxious person.

A few weeks before the October 2017 sessions of general conference, I spoke with Jill about our quest for perfection and its relationship to grace. Jill is a lovely mother of four who tearfully explained what it's like to burden yourself with fear that you'll never be good enough, especially as compared to others and to Heavenly Father's expectations of us.

JANE: "Do you think those comparisons create deeper perfectionistic tendencies?"

JILL: "Oh yeah. . . . When you compare yourself to what you view as the perfect mother, if you have a friend or an acquaintance or somebody you know that it seems like they've got it good and you compare yourself to that, it's almost debilitating. Logically I know that they don't have a perfect life, but from my view it seems like they do, so I'm trying to achieve that too. It just never happens."

JANE: "But that's really not the message of the gospel—so why do we still do this to ourselves?"

JILL: "I think because we know that we're trying to achieve being like our Heavenly Father, and He's a perfect being. I guess I feel responsibility that way. Knowing that causes us to feel like we should and could be doing better. I think we can. I just know that it puts pressures on me personally to do more. I feel like I always need to be doing more so that I can be the type of person that I feel like Heavenly Father wants me to be."

JANE: "Do you ever think that He's happy with who you are right now?"

JILL: "Now I'm going to start crying. . . . No, I know there have been times when I know that He loves me. But no, I don't feel like I'm as good as what He expects me to be."

JANE: "Why do you feel that way?"

JILL: "Because I can see all of my flaws. I know what He was like. I know what Christ was like, and I see all the areas where I just don't measure up."

Jill evoked feelings I had struggled to articulate during my darkest days of depression and echoed the feelings many others shared about negative self-talk, comparisons, and failure. It is daunting to contemplate the nuanced diplomacy often demanded to gently urge people to move away from these feelings without discounting their genuine concerns and fears. The difficulty of it should not, however, inhibit us from trying.

A few weeks after my conversation with Jill, Elder Holland concluded his general conference remarks by saying this:

"Brothers and sisters, every one of us aspires to a more Christlike life than we often succeed in living. If we admit that honestly and are trying to improve, we're not hypocrites; we're human. May we refuse to let our own mortal follies and the inevitable shortcomings of even the best men and women around us make us cynical about . . . our hope for the future, or the possibility of godliness. If we persevere, then somewhere in eternity our refinement will be finished and complete, which is the New Testament meaning of perfection. I testify of that grand destiny made available to us by the Atonement of the Lord Jesus Christ, who Himself continued from grace to grace until in His immortality He received a perfect fulness of celestial glory."

Elder Holland had barely returned to his seat that Saturday morning when I received this email from Jill:

"One of the questions you asked me was if anyone could say anything that would make me feel differently about how I felt about myself and perfectionism (or something like that). I answered 'No.'

"I was wrong. The talk Elder Holland just gave in conference touched me to the core. I have never had anyone be able to describe what 'being perfect' means in the scriptures like he just did."

A MOTHER-AND-SON PERSPECTIVE: CAROL AND TIM

Carol's son, Tim, who suffers from depression, had similar challenges with perfectionism. Carol acknowledged her own struggles with how she might have contributed to that:

CAROL (SPEAKING ABOUT TIM): "His standard was so high—partly from me. I've been a black-and-white person until the last fifteen years. I expected perfection from [the children]. It wasn't the Church and our ward, it was me. Achieve, achieve, achieve. Up before school to practice the piano. He got the message. He didn't get the other part, that we still love you no matter what."

JANE: "Given what you've been through, looking back, how would you have parented differently?"

CAROL: "I would have had high expectations but I would have had more love and tenderness and quiet talk and more trust. . . . I feel like I've been through my own Gethsemane. Now, I have great compassion for everybody."

TIM (CAROL'S SON): "Yes, [this experience] has helped me realize that turning to the Savior with faith in His atoning sacrifice to overcome our weaknesses is a process . . . and we will never overcome completely and fully in this life. I have to accept that I'm imperfect, and that's okay. No matter how strictly I follow the rules: reading my scriptures, saying my prayers, going to church, paying tithing, volunteering for everything that I'm asked to do at church . . . those aren't the things that are going to get me to salvation. They don't save me right now. I don't have to be as rigid and expect so much of myself; if I do have shortcomings, that's okay. They can be made up for by the Savior. I don't have to beat myself up about them in this life or in this moment."

THE STRAIGHT SCOOP ON BEING PERFECT

As Tim learned, perfection is not expected in the here and now but is something we attain *hereafter, through the grace of Jesus Christ.* Joseph Smith taught that those who will be brought forth in the Resurrection of the just are "they who are just men *made* perfect through Jesus the mediator of the new covenant, who wrought out this perfect atonement through the shedding of his own blood" (Doctrine and Covenants 76:69; emphasis added).

Without the Savior, it is impossible for any man or woman to become perfect. It's not an objective we can achieve on our own! In fact, the Savior Himself—who was without sin on this earth—did not claim eternal perfection until *after* His Resurrection. In the Sermon on the Mount He told His disciples: "Be ye therefore perfect, even as your *Father* which is in heaven is perfect" (Matthew 5:48; emphasis added). It was *after* He had atoned for our sins and risen again in glory that He included Himself as a perfected being with the Father, proclaiming to the Nephites: "I would that ye should be perfect *even as I,* or your Father who is in heaven is perfect" (3 Nephi 12:48; emphasis added).

The footnote connected to the word *perfect* in 3 Nephi 12:48 refers us to Matthew 5:48, with its own accompanying footnote that defines the word *perfect* as meaning *complete, finished, fully developed.* President Russell M. Nelson has interpreted the verses and surrounding doctrine of perfection as follows: "The term *perfect* was translated from the Greek *teleios,* which means 'complete.' . . . The infinitive form of the verb is *teleiono,* which means 'to reach a distant end, to be fully developed, to consummate, or to finish.' Please note that the word does not imply 'freedom from error'; it implies 'achieving a distant objective.' . . .

"We need not be dismayed if our earnest efforts toward perfection now seem so arduous and endless. Perfection is pending. It can come in full only after the Resurrection and only through the Lord. It awaits all who love him and keep his commandments."

There is no doctrine in The Church of Jesus Christ of Latter-day Saints requiring perfection here and now! Yet many of us have appropriated the Savior's command as a modern-day call to be without flaw—in appearance, in academics, in business, in parenting, in lesson planning, in fitness, in every area of life we can think of. Social media fuels the flames as we scroll through Instagram and Facebook feeds carefully filtered and curated to show only the happiest, prettiest, and shiniest of events in the lives of our family and friends. We drive past billboards that remind us of our flaws while extolling the latest trends in plastic surgery. "Make your inner beauty jealous!" proclaims one on a stretch of I-15 in Utah County. "Friends don't let friends muffin-top" states another across the country in Jackson, Michigan. "Be the envy of your neighborhood," is plastered on another near downtown Salt Lake City.

BEING INSTEAD OF DOING: ALLY'S DISCOVERY

Ally, a fellow recovering perfectionist, knows all too well that this glut—the billboards, the social media posts, the airbrushed magazine ads—of unrealistic ideals that we nevertheless believe we have to achieve is overwhelming and not only feeds but fosters depression. She has redefined perfectionism, saying: "I've come to the conclusion that I would now define perfectionism not as being perfect but about constantly fearing that you're not enough. . . . If you're in constant worry or fear that you're not enough, then what are you? A perfectionist."

Ally has dealt with chronic depression for years while also battling an autoimmune disease and, during at least one season, a heavy bout of toxic perfectionism. Twice during those years she has also served as a ward Relief Society president. The first time was amazing, she said. It was as if the depression and autoimmune symptoms lifted just so she could fulfill the calling and do all the things that needed doing. She felt great while serving and was optimistic that, with faith, she would feel the same way the second time around, even though she was confined to bed when she received the call.

Perhaps you can guess how that worked out. This time, Ally experienced no relief from either the depression or the autoimmune disease. She found that she could *do* very little. And her inner perfectionist constantly bombarded her with feelings of inadequacy and self-reproach. She muddled on for a while until she reached her breaking point.

"I had such severe depression by then and I couldn't feel the Spirit anymore. I knew that I could not be Relief Society president and not feel the Spirit. There were too many decisions that had to be made. I called the bishop and basically, I quit. I quit being the Relief Society president. I joke about that now, but there's so much pressure to never quit. . . . You feel like such a failure.

"You start thinking that no matter what you're given in life, it's like, if I have this depression I'll never be able to accomplish anything. I'll never be who I want to be. I'll never reach what I thought was possible."

Ally sank into a deeper depression for eight months, saying it was only her husband's love and support that sustained her and helped her to finally accept that she might not be able to be a doer for the time being, but she could still *be*. She was still a mom and a wife, and there were some things she could *be* from bed. She could still find joy in her children. She could study and learn.

"At first, I not only lost my identity, but I lost my power to *do*. Losing all of that at once, you feel like, 'Who am I? What am I? What can I even do here to make a difference?' I decided there were a few things that I could still do. One thing that I particularly enjoy is intelligence—learning new things and feeling that joy of light and understanding of things.

"Sometimes you're just too sick to do anything, and that's fine, but other times you are healthy enough to sit up in bed and you can still read poetry and you can still read your scriptures and you can still learn from good books. . . . When my kids would get home from school I would try to tell them stories or things like that. It's like my influence became very small, but it was still an influence in those little ways.

"The one thing that I feel like in those years maybe saved my family—I recognize this so strongly—is that though my mom was a doer, I don't ever remember her sitting down with me and playing a game or talking to me. I don't mind that, because I was a doer too. Every single day the kids were in and out of my bed. Each one of them would come and spend twenty minutes with me or more. I would sit and talk to them—each of them individually—because that's all I could do. The relationships that I developed with my children and still have with my children are things that I never would have had if I was still a doer."

AVOIDING "DEBILITATING COMPARISONS": TALIA'S EXPERIENCE

I am hopeful that the drive for perfection in the present will change from comparing ourselves to others and decrying our shortcomings to accepting who we are and committing to give our best effort to be more Christlike. I love the story Talia shares about being reminded to do this. Talia has a PhD in molecular biology, a field that requires extreme precision and skill—perfection, really—in some tasks in the laboratory. It's a profession that suits her well because she has always pushed herself to excel. It's a field in which it's okay—mandatory, even—to expect perfection in some areas.

Sometimes Talia has found the drive for perfection spilling into other parts of her life and throwing her for a loop. The challenge in perfectionism is that "you find yourself constantly comparing yourself to someone else." When this happens, she says, it's easy to feel debilitated and beat yourself up as you simultaneously pass judgment on the person you're comparing yourself with. She shares this personal experience:

"After Lucas was born, I took him to his four-week appointment. I'll be honest, I looked awful. I rolled out of bed after a long night of breastfeeding just in time to strap Lucas into his car seat. We barely arrived on time for the morning appointment. I was wearing worn-out maternity clothes, very little makeup, and had my hair in a bun when Lucas decided to add to my 'beauty' by spitting up all over me so that my shirt was drenched.

"While we were waiting for our appointment, another mom walked in with a baby that was obviously much younger than mine, and she looked amazing. Her hair and makeup were done, her clothes were so cute, and her baby was dressed in something other than pajamas. I overheard her saying that her baby was only five days old. I couldn't believe how amazing she looked. I felt so ugly I wanted to hide.

"A few days after the appointment, I called my sister and told her about the experience, and she reprimanded me for my feelings. She reminded me that it was a miracle that Lucas and I had even survived childbirth (I had to have an emergency C-section after both my uterus and bladder tore during delivery) and that I was well enough to drive to the appointment, since I still had a catheter in place to allow my bladder to heal. She also said that I knew nothing about this other mom and that it was possible that she had a nanny or family members to help with the baby and maybe even a night nurse to help with feedings. It was unfair to judge both the other mom and myself and try to 'run faster than I had strength'" (see Mosiah 4:27).

For Talia, this was a pointed reminder about her own worth as well as the worth of the mother she had compared herself to. Sharing the incident with a trusted ally—her sister—helped her put words to her feelings. And talking through it reminded her that she was doing the best she could and that we never know what another individual is struggling with, no matter how perfect his or her life looks on the outside.

Most of what we see is, in fact, only what people choose to present. We have no way of knowing the personal details, struggles, and imperfections of another person or family. I love the story Elder Gary E. Stevenson told at the BYU Women's Conference in May 2017. He held up a lovely picture of his own family—parents and children smiling happily in color-coordinated outfits. He then described what was happening behind the scenes and behind the smiles: first, he had forgotten about the appointment entirely and left his wife on her own to get their four boys groomed and ready; second, one son had worn white athletic socks with dress pants and was thus covering his ankle with a strategically placed hand; third, another son had stumbled while waiting for him to arrive and incurred a bloody nose that had dripped all over his white turtleneck, which he was now wearing backwards; fourth, yet another son had only recently recovered from a crying fit after his brother had thrown an apple at him. And that wasn't the whole story, either.

If that picture had been posted on social media today (it was taken long before Facebook and Instagram), all we would see in the image is "a family of four lovely, well-behaved boys, color coordinated, enjoying a harmonious family photo opportunity together," Elder Stevenson said. He called it an "idealized reality" and went on to say: "Generally speaking, pictures that get posted on social media tend to portray life in the very best and often in an unrealistic way. They are often filled with beautiful images of home decor, wonderful vacation spots, and elaborate food preparation. The danger, of course, is that many become discouraged that they seemingly don't measure up to this 'idealized virtual reality.'" When you don't measure up to impossible ideals, he says, therein lie the pitfalls of succumbing to "debilitating comparisons."

The Savior compares us to no one. "For the Lord seeth not as man seeth; for man looketh on the outward appearance, but the Lord looketh on the heart" (1 Samuel 16:7).

IDENTIFYING SATAN'S COUNTERFEIT: KARA'S TESTIMONY

It's important that we don't forget that striving for the eternal perfection of which the Savior speaks is not only worthwhile but also a commandment. The key is discernment, recognizing that the Savior wants us to succeed and makes it possible for us to do so. It is Satan who teaches the counterfeit of immediate perfection and rejoices when we declare ourselves failures for not accomplishing the impossible.

"We all have an innate desire to be good and to do good things by working hard," says psychologist Janet Scharman, former vice president of Student Life at Brigham Young University. "The problem comes when we feel a false sense of urgency that we must get it all right, right now. We begin to believe that God's blessings to us will be withheld until we can earn our reward. Associated with this is Satan's lie that we can, and perhaps somehow must, do it entirely on our own without God's help. As a result, this strategy works on two dysfunctional beliefs. It ignores the 'work in progress' aspect of achieving perfection, while it also sadly, carefully leads us away from reliance on God's loving interventions. What results as we move in this direction is an overwhelming feeling that we must be perfectly in control of our own behaviors, our environment, and those closest to us."

Kara is bright, thoughtful, and filled with the Spirit; I could sense it from our first conversation. Kara also has experience battling Satan's lie that we must do everything on our own.

Kara's depression began with exhaustion and dark days of shame. Equally difficult were the intense negativity and hostility that accompanied them. "I would be at church," she says, "and I would feel like . . . this perfect person I was being asked to live up to was so difficult and so unattainable that I started to have feelings of resentment, which was unexpected. And when I was around other Mormon women that seemed to have everything together I would be really angry at them, or really resentful, or really frustrated because I felt like they had something that I could never have because I was irreparably broken."

In her journal she wrote that "depression would creep in during quiet moments, lie down with me, and cozy up for months at a time.

It wreaked havoc on my mind and soul, and eventually my body, through doubts and fears that consumed, loneliness that turned to anger and resentment towards people I loved (and also people I didn't know), hard-hearted drudgery in going to church, and the added weight of failure as my responsibilities overwhelmed me and perfectionism suffocated me."

When she thought about sharing her feelings, she would hear these words over and over again in her mind: "Others will know! They will judge you and think you're less-than! They will see that you're not perfect and all your faults will be known!"

Kara was trapped, more insecure—and more depressed—with every thought and worry. Although being in church meetings became a real struggle for her, she continued to attend, isolating herself in the back and leaving with her family as quickly as possible when meetings ended. But then one day came a small turning point.

"I was at church," she says, "and I was listening to one of my friends bear her testimony. She talked about Third Nephi, chapter 17, where Christ appears to the Nephites. He blesses the children . . . then He turns to the people and expresses great compassion for them. He says, 'Have ye any that are lame, or blind, or halt, or maimed, or leprous, or that are withered, or that are deaf, or that are *afflicted in any manner?* Bring them hither and I will heal them.' I remember sitting in that meeting and thinking, 'Oh my gosh, that's me. I am afflicted in a manner, and He can heal me.' That was the first time I felt hope."

Kara began to confide in others: her husband, a doctor, a therapist. As she received help, her depression lightened, and divine light flowed back into her life. And although she didn't recognize it at the time, the things she learned as she healed and allowed the Savior's light to illuminate her not only prepared her for her next episode of depression but also helped her reach out to others and share their burdens.

"Perfectionists," Kara says, "we deal in the black and white. There's no gray area. It's all or nothing. And that's Satan's plan. Heavenly Father wants us to live in the gray areas where there's mercy and love, compassion, charity."

A little more than a year after Kara and I first spoke, she sent me an email, updating me on her life and her progress and an important lesson she had learned:

"I feel like I was very cavalier when we spoke before because I was in a 'depression remission' of sorts. I thought I had walked through the fire and come out on the other side all the wiser. Ha! That is laughable! The worst of it was yet to come. And still I'm here and, I think, much wiser. And what I've found is the more often I tell of my experience, the more capable I am of managing my illness. And I think it's because of the connectedness it creates between myself and those I speak with. Of course there is medication and some therapy involved, but a major part of my wellness plan includes emotional honesty (not shying away from talking about it) and daily interaction with other women. As I strive to do this, I am amazed at how many women are happy and relieved when I openly discuss my limitations. Many of them suffer from depression in some form or another and for a variety of reasons. It still surprises me the number of women like me out there, all of us plugging away in parallel lives and yet not knowing that we sorrow in secret in unison. . . .

"I remember my Relief Society president pulling me aside a few years ago and telling me in confidence that there was a woman among us feeling depressed and severely alone. She asked if I would reach out to this sister and sit by her during the meetings. Naturally, I was happy to do so and felt compassion already for this woman. But when she told me who this sister was, I almost gasped audibly because it was someone whom I felt was well liked and friendly, happy and productive. And yet she suffered inside where no one saw it."

Christ works through us as we accept Him and God the Father as the architects and ourselves as the builders. Learning to be vulnerable and show up *as we are* can be painful, but it fosters humility, teaches us beautiful lessons, and contributes to the building of the kingdom of God.

I have a special affection for the story of the Lord visiting in the house of Mary and Martha; I think many of us do. We see ourselves in the overwhelmed Martha, in her anxious fuss to provide a perfect house and meal. We even see ourselves in her petty, misguided criticism of her sister, a habit we may also have that fuels our insecurity about our own performance in life. We long for the Lord's assurance that our stressful perfectionism is unnecessary, that He accepts us as we are. Here it is:

"Martha, Martha, thou art careful and troubled about many things: But one thing is needful: and Mary hath chosen that good part, which shall not be taken away from her" (Luke 10:41–42).

We need to live the message of this story, for our own good *and* the benefit of others. Instead of being "careful and troubled about many things," struggling to keep up appearances while at the same time judging the failings of others, we should strive for that one needful thing—to come unto Christ and allow Him to save us—and liberate our fellow Marthas to do the same. The Savior already knows about our anxiety, our depression, our worry, our fear, our tendency to give up when we can't be perfect in every way. He knows it all. And He loves us anyway! Because of that love, there is hope—hope that the Atonement will take care of our imperfections and make us whole, or perfect, in His time.

That is the miracle of the gospel and the essence of the Atonement:

The Lord knows our potential and what we can become. He does not expect perfection because He knows it's impossible at this stage in our lives. What He expects is progress; His grace covers the rest.

That brings me to another miraculous element in all of this: the grace offered us through the Atonement—the Savior's grace—actually works to change how we believe and feel about ourselves if we let it. Professor Daniel K Judd, a psychologist and the associate dean of Religion at Brigham Young University, conducted a study of 574 BYU students with respect to their experience with legalism, grace, and various measures of mental health. "We found that the more the respondents believed that their salvation was primarily a result of *their own good works* (legalism), the higher were their scores on measures of shame, anxiety, depression, and obsessive-compulsive behavior (scrupulosity). When we examined the influence of grace with these same students, we found that those who *understood and embraced the principle of grace* had dramatically lower scores on these same measures." It is truly astounding what the Savior's grace can and does cover!

"I GIVE MYSELF GRACE"

Jackie is a young military wife with three very young daughters. During early motherhood, her husband was frequently deployed, and quite often she found herself alone, full of anxiety and some depression as she tried to make everything around her perfect. She felt as if she'd hit rock bottom. Then something changed. Little by little, she came out of the depression. Medication helped, but so did natural methods of healing and—perhaps most importantly, she says—grace. Over and over again when I was talking with Jackie, she said four words: "I give myself grace."

"Our only hope for true perfection is in receiving it as a gift from heaven—we can't 'earn' it. Thus, the grace of Christ offers us not only salvation from sorrow and sin and death but also salvation from our own persistent self-criticism," says Elder Holland. If the Savior can give us grace, then surely we can each give ourselves a little bit of grace. The Savior would have it no other way, for it is grace that brings us back to Him and allows Him—and others—to see on the outside what we are inside. It is, after all, that very grace that will perfect us in the end.

CHAPTER 5

KIDNAPPED SOULS: YOUNG PEOPLE AND DEPRESSION

Even the youths shall faint and be weary.

—ISAIAH 40:30

For me, the face of teenage depression will always be Cece,* a lovely young woman I knew from church who providentially stopped and rang my doorbell one cold January morning when she was on her way to jump off a bridge.

In children and teenagers like Cece, depression manifests itself in unique ways. Sadness is not always a visible component, and those symptoms that *are* noticeable can easily be confused with what we label as typical teenage angst: irritability, rash anger, and a desire to be left alone. Parents, teachers, and even medical professionals can easily misread the signs. Because teenagers' brains are still developing, they may not have the words to describe what they are feeling or the life experience to contextualize those feelings. Young people are more likely than adults to act out aggressively, to cut or injure themselves, and to experiment with drugs, alcohol, and sex; their behavior is riskier. While all teenagers can be moody, psychologists Jeanne Segal and Melinda Smith note that "depression is something different. Depression can destroy the very essence of a teenager's personality."

*Name has been changed.

75

When I talked to the parents of depressed children, the same scenarios, even the same language, came up again and again:

"He would sleep hours and hours and hours and hours. As soon as he would come home from school in the afternoon, he'd go to bed, wake up and eat dinner about nine, and then go right back to bed."

"At first, the nightly meltdowns were unsettling. As they continued, I realized this wasn't normal behavior but I didn't know what to do. My daughter needed me by her side, but everything I tried to do was all wrong. I was desperate to help her through the tears and terror of anxiety, but crippled by my inexperience and lack of resources."

"Until sixth grade, he was a straight-A student. Everything he touched turned to gold. But starting in junior high he just . . . went downhill. He couldn't keep up with assignments; he started not wanting to go to school."

"She just took the car. Didn't even have a permit yet. Still hasn't said why or where she was going. She crashed into a wall just outside the neighborhood."

"She's really hard to live with. She's angry a lot of the time. She is selfish, and it's really hard to separate and think and remember when you are dealing with her on a day-to-day basis that this is a product of depression. . . . It's hard not to take it personally."

For doctors, these similarities are symptoms—the telltale signs of a devastating disease. For parents, they are steps on a personal Via Dolorosa, where each station is a place of unimaginable anguish.

"She had this whole part of herself that she had completely locked me out from, and it was so terrifying. . . . I am her mother, how do I not even know about this?"

"It was like he was falling over the edge of a cliff and we couldn't do anything to stop it."

"Here is a kid who should be able to go wherever he wants to college because he is so smart. Here is a kid who excels in music and athletics, whatever he wants to do . . . and now he is doing none of those things. He is doing none of them. That was just so hard to let go of. We know he is capable of so much and yet we also recognize that because of mental illness he is not going to be able to do any of those things and it's okay. It's not his fault. It doesn't make him a bad person, but it's still so hard and so painful to just let it go.

"He was eighteen at the beginning of the senior year and as graduation is coming his friends are getting mission calls and the questions begin: 'Does he have his papers in? What's his plan?' For a while you just say, 'Oh, no. He is going to try school first' or whatever. Now I'm at the point I just tell people he struggles with mental illness and a mission really isn't an option for him. That was a big turning point for me too because as he was going downhill I thought, 'Oh, this is not boding well for a mission.' . . .

"When he went away to college and things fell apart I just realized, 'No, he can't serve a mission. He is just not capable.'"

For Latter-day Saints there is unique grief associated with the experience of parenting a depressed young person (not to mention being one): feelings of failure when missionary service or temple marriage becomes unlikely, and stigmatization for failing to meet our dauntingly high expectations.

"It's funny with the Church," one parent told me. "I'm not saying that I don't believe in the prophet. I do. But sometimes I hear things like we should be the happiest of people, we should be cheerful in everything we do because we have the truth. Sometimes I don't want to go to church because someone is going to ask me how I'm doing and I'm afraid I will start to cry and say, 'Oh, things are horrible at my house. You have no idea.' When you have high expectations, there is going to be additional pain when those expectations are not met."

Shelley, like other parents of LGBTQ+ children, daily wrestles with the knowledge that her gay son has an elevated risk of suicide. She expresses both the complexity of the struggle and the source of hope. "I think that a lot of his anxiety and depression stems from the sexuality. . . . I think that he's always talked about, 'I'm going to serve a mission. I'm going to get married in the temple,' all these plans that he had, and as he got older, and went through puberty, I guess, all of a sudden, he's like, 'Oh crap. What's going on? How can I still do all of the things that I always wanted to do and thought I was going to do?'

"I've seen depression in him like crazy, and that's one of the reasons I want him to be out. My inclination is tell the whole world because keeping secrets makes people miserable. My personal feeling is that if you feel like you can't let people know who you really are, then you feel completely isolated, then you're far more likely to commit suicide.

"What we've told him is that life is long, Heavenly Father knows him, the plan of salvation is true, and he has eternity to work it out."

Another mother I interviewed spoke of her daughter's worry that God hated her: "Lily would come to me and say, 'I've been praying so much for God to take this away and I've been trying to read extra scriptures every night to make this go away and I've been trying to do extra Personal Progress goals,' and when she was actually well enough to do any of this she'd worry: 'And nothing is working, Mom. How come God isn't helping me like He's supposed to?'"

Their stories—and I have heard hundreds of them from parents and children alike—are a litany of pain, confusion, crushing disappointment, and unbearable loneliness. Being depressed is like being "in solitary confinement, mandated solitary confinement," as one teen put it to me. The parents of depressed teens often feel the same way. After all, it's pretty common to gather with a group of moms and discuss your toddlers' destructive phases involving boxes of cereal and chewed-up board books; but to discuss your teen's self-destructive behavior is fraught with stigma, not to mention a violation of your child's privacy. Indeed, parents of mentally ill children often feel entirely alone.

Remarkably, though, when these teenagers and their parents *do* share their stories, and you listen to them closely—I mean *really* listen, with an ear that is attuned to testimony—many of them also bear witness to the miraculous power of the Savior's Atonement. Even when depression becomes so oppressive that the Spirit appears to have been utterly usurped by a chemically unbalanced brain and mind, you can still see glimpses of God's love. This is not to deny that far too many of these stories end tragically. But the possibility of healing and grace is always there. The stories that follow are a witness to that power.

CLAIRE: FINDING HIGHLIGHTS IN THE SHADOWS

Claire's* depression began—as it does for many children and teens—with anxiety. In fact, nearly half of teens who suffer from depression will also suffer from an anxiety disorder. The National Institute of Mental Health reports that 31.9 percent of teens aged thirteen to eighteen dealt with a diagnosable anxiety disorder from 2001 to 2004. And 8.3 percent of those teens dealt with severe anxiety.

"I didn't really feel normal anymore," Claire says of the time around her fourteenth year, before her diagnosis. Her mother, Rose,* also remembers a change—she could see it in her daughter's eyes.

After several weeks and a number of difficult conversations, Rose discovered a small part of what Claire was feeling. "She told us that she was experiencing panic attacks. And I thought, 'How do you even know what a panic attack is? You're only fourteen.'"

Claire described feeling shaky and sweaty. Her heart would race, and sometimes she'd feel like her chest was being crushed. After a physical exam by a general practitioner, she was diagnosed with mild

*Name has been changed.

depression, and an antidepressant was prescribed. Rose was hopeful that the medication would provide a quick fix, that within a few weeks that dead look in her daughter's eyes would go away and she would return to normal. Instead, Claire's academic work nose-dived; she grew irritable and angry and began spending most of her time by herself.

As Claire increasingly isolated herself, she also worried more what others would think if they knew how all-encompassing her pain was. "It got really pretty bad, to a point where there was so much inside of me that I didn't want to be inside of me anymore. I didn't know how to take it out of myself. I just knew there had to be something physical that would take it out."

Claire cut herself to gain relief from the storm raging in her mind. Each cut released some of that pain in a very physical way. "It was validating," she told me, "because I could see, 'Okay, there is pain, it's not just in my brain, I'm not making it up. It's an actual thing. It's here.'"

Research into self-harm is in the early stages, but doctors and parents alike find that it does not always indicate a suicidal teen. Usually the teen is hurting himself—or, more commonly, herself—as a way to release unwanted emotions. Clinicians call this behavior non-suicidal self-injury (NSSI). A 2012 study published in the journal *Pediatrics* found that ninth-grade girls (the age Claire was when she began cutting herself) are at the highest risk for NSSI. In fact, almost one out of five (19 percent) of ninth-grade girls admit to injuring themselves. But Claire's suicidal thoughts were quite real. "I never admitted to myself, 'I want to die,' or, 'I want to kill myself,'" she told me. "It was more, 'I want to escape,' or, 'I want to fall asleep and never wake up' . . . not in a death way, but I just want to escape."

Claire's parents pulled her from school temporarily so she could undergo four weeks of outpatient treatment at a local mental-health facility. Leaving her at the hospital each day, her mother recalled, brought home a new reality. "I had known about depression on this very superficial, textbook level, but not living it and breathing it and seeing someone suffer from it. . . . It was really scary."

The costs were daunting: $12,000 for the program, and it was next to impossible to find the right doctors to treat Claire once she'd finished it. Rose made dozens and dozens of calls to psychiatrists. Anyone who specialized in adolescent depression was booked. Rose felt helpless and frustrated. "I think typically in our Latter-day Saint community, so much of everything is talking to your fellow ward members. Who do you use for your electrician? Where do you get your hair cut? But you don't really want to talk about this. I felt like a failure as a mom, that I did something wrong, and I also didn't want to embarrass Claire."

Fortunately, Claire was able to continue seeing the therapist from the program on a private basis. After more setbacks, recovery began, but it was painfully slow, and, truthfully, Claire is a different person than she was before anxiety and depression struck.

Depression has no quick fix, Rose says. "It's taken me a long time to realize that. I think I was just always waiting for the next thing to be the magic cure that would fix it. It's just taken me such a long time to realize that this is who Claire is."

Rose worries how Claire feels now that she has faced some of the toughest aspects of the disease. Has her spirit suffered? Does she feel the love of fellow Church members and friends, let alone the love of her Heavenly Father? "I want her to feel safe enough in the Church and in the gospel to feel like she can struggle with depression and anxiety and still be a good member of the Church and still be connected to the gospel and have faith in Christ."

Claire was startlingly frank about this and about how she was doing in her treatment in general. It's also where she identified hope—or the highlights, as she calls them—in her story of depression and its dark, frightening shadows.

CLAIRE: "When I started treatment, I was very adamant to not allow the Spirit or God to heal me. I was going to heal myself. I'm a really stubborn person."

Like many of us, Claire was committed to a program of "self-rescue," viewing her religion, the Atonement, even the Lord Himself as extraneous, perhaps even detrimental, to the process. "I felt like I was the only one who could save myself, and nothing else could be real while I was trying to save myself or else I would get distracted."

JANE: "Has your thought process about that changed since you've been in treatment, or is it still ongoing?"

CLAIRE: "It's definitely still ongoing. I have times when I'm mad at God or mad at the Church because it didn't help me when I was going through all of this. Then I remember that I was not *letting* it help me. I was labeling myself. I was like, 'Oh, you're a freak. You're hearing voices in your head telling you you're fat. That's weird, that's . . . I don't know. That's psychotic.' I was really mean to myself. It took me a long time to realize that people aren't as mean to you as you are to yourself."

Claire says she has to remind herself frequently that we all have trials and that trials can make her stronger. She has created a particularly lovely metaphor to help her work through what it means to be depressed and exist in her "new" state of being.

"Honestly, this is going to be so cheesy," she says, "but it's like when you're painting a seascape, especially the beach. The painting contains a lot of shadows and highlights and a lot of detail."

She points out that you have to step back to see the whole thing. Without the highlights, the painting would be flat and dark; without the shadows, the images in a painting are not anchored to anything.

The light in a painting cannot be emphasized without some darkness to frame it and draw the eye toward it. "Everything," Claire says, including the shadows and highlights, "has to come together to make something wonderful. I think art and music are highlights of my life and depression is a shadow. I need highlights and shadows. I need highlights and shadows to be a whole person."

JANE: "That's really poignant, thank you. Is there anything else that I have not asked you that you would like to add?"

CLAIRE: "I really want to say, 'Just don't be afraid.' I know that sounds invalidating, because obviously, I was so afraid, and if someone had just told me like, 'Don't be afraid,' then it would not have been helpful. But like when my mom first found out that I self-harmed? I was so afraid. I was so scared, but she wasn't angry. Nobody's going to be angry that you're feeling sad. Nobody's going to be angry that you want to die. Nobody's going to be angry that you feel fat. They're just going to want to love you, so don't be afraid of people's reactions. Just know that people aren't as mean as you think they are. People aren't as mean as you are to yourself."

ISABELA: HOPE AND EMPATHY ON THE OTHER SIDE OF DEPRESSION

Like Claire's, Isabela's* depression first manifested as anxiety, hitting during her seventh-grade year of school. Her mom, Luiza,* remembers it coming on suddenly. The only signs that anything was off-kilter masked themselves as the typical worries and changes that accompany the move to middle school and making new friends. One day Isabela seemed fine, the next, "I really felt like her soul had been kidnapped from her," Luiza says.

"All of her ability to experience joy and happiness and laughter

*Name has been changed.

and pleasure was gone, had been taken away. She had none of that any longer. All that was left was the part that could experience fear and terror and anxiety and sorrow and pain and suffering and sadness. . . . She was so sensitive, both physically and emotionally, to anything around her. It was as though you had burned off her skin. Everything was painful. Everything was difficult, and so she just spent hours crying and despondent."

Today, Isabela is an adult. That out-of-the-blue tornado of anxiety and depression struck fifteen years ago. She describes herself before that time as a cheerful, happy kid. "There had been no sexual assault, no abuse," she says. "I had good parents and a safe place to live, and there was always food on the table. Lots of love and acceptance." Like physical diseases—cancer and diabetes, for example— depression in children and teens can sneak up suddenly, often silently. Changes in mood, irritability, and anger can all initially be attributed to something else: puberty, hormones, PMS, troubles at school or with friends. It's not unlike the headaches, fatigue, and weight loss that are brushed off as stress related or just part of life in general before the words *cancer* or *chronic disease* are uttered.

The unraveling that is depression can come on swift and strong. "In the depths of my depression," Isabela says, "I had moved into the basement of our house and was sleeping on a mat and was not eating anything and did not want to leave the house. I did not want to see any friends. I was not sleeping well and I felt like there was no point to any of it, that nobody liked me. . . . Strangely, a small part of me recognized that this was not normal, but the overwhelming part of my brain was telling me that there was no purpose to anything. I remember really wanting to sleep until the pain went away. I didn't want to kill myself. . . . I wanted to just sleep and never wake up until I was better."

A few months after my interview with Isabela and her mom, they found a journal Isabela had kept during that time of illness. Despite the years that have intervened, it is still painful to read the words: one huge letter per page, spelling out "I hate myself." As a middle schooler, Isabela felt particularly vulnerable. Despite being in treatment, she simply didn't feel like she could go back to school after this first episode. What would the other kids think? Would they say she was crazy? Would they mock her? Bully her? What would her teachers think? Would they doubt her intelligence? Would they treat her differently? She missed an entire year of school, adding another discouraging complication to treating her disease.

Suddenly, happiness and success seemed out of reach. Luiza says they felt like they needed to hold a funeral for Isabela to mourn the parts of her that were gone and might never come back. All of the good parts of her seemed lost. It stretched credulity to think she might ever go to college. "All of a sudden it went from where I was thinking she had such a bright future and she was so capable and so loving and lovable and wonderful and I could imagine so many good things for her . . . to wondering whether she would survive or whether she would be able to graduate from high school," Luiza says.

A breakthrough occurred when a phenomenal therapist trained in cognitive behavioral therapy began working with Isabela. Their personalities clicked, and Isabela began improving. Antidepressants and antianxiety medications also played a role in recovery. Finding the right medications and the correct dosage took time, as did continued involvement with a psychiatrist and other mental-health specialists.

Of course, during this time of slow and gradual improvement, life at home had to continue. The families of those who suffer from depression can't simply stop carrying on with their lives. Parenting takes on a whole new dimension when a child is afflicted with depression. Financial and logistical constraints can mean fewer opportunities for parents to connect with their children who aren't depressed. And the eggshells parents often traverse in dealing with depressed teenagers become increasingly fragile. For Luiza, it was a balancing act. She had to learn when to soothe and when to be more demanding, when to insist that Isabela practice what she'd learned in therapy or to simply require her to come up from the basement and participate in family life.

Today, Isabela gratefully reflects on her parents' devoted efforts. She remembers one of her initial visits to a psychiatrist that almost didn't happen because she refused to leave the basement. "They made this appointment," she says, "with the psychiatrist and I said, 'I'm not going.' My dad just physically picked me up and carried me to the physician's office, and I spent that office visit sitting in the corner crying and not talking to her at all."

It was a low point for Isabela, but she continued therapy, sometimes only because her parents forced her to, and her health improved. For her parents, when to insist and when to let something go was a matter of guesswork. The one thing that became nonnegotiable, however, was being honest with themselves and their children about what they were facing, and then facing it head-on. Experts recommend full disclosure with children when one of their siblings suffers from a chronic illness, including depression. Dr. Esther Dechant of McLean Hospital and Harvard Medical School says not to pretend everything is okay in an attempt to "protect" the other children. "Kids instinctively know when something is wrong with a sibling and will have many questions," she says. "Not talking about it will only make them wonder more, which can cause anxiety and fear as their imaginations run wild with possible answers. Talking openly about their sibling's depression . . . inviting them to ask questions and share their feelings . . . will not only reassure them that their sibling is being helped but will also destigmatize the illness."

Dr. Dechant also recommends keeping a close eye on siblings.

"Everyone in the family will be affected in some way when a child is battling depression. 'Healthy' children may feel ignored, anxious, or confused. Individualized attention, or even professional counseling, can help them understand and manage their feelings about the situation."

Finally, it's important for parents to take care of themselves and, particularly, to avoid the blame game. When abuse and neglect are not in the equation, parents are not to blame for a child's mental illness. A child is never to blame for having depression. Floundering in the thick fog of depression, it's often difficult for sufferers not to feel guilty, blame themselves, and feel entirely abandoned.

The resources—physical, financial, emotional, and spiritual—of families with a child, or children, suffering from mental illness are often stretched exceedingly thin. Many parents describe extreme strain associated with even the most pragmatic aspects of their children's illness. "I made thirty phone calls and two of them returned my phone call and said, 'I'm sorry, we're not taking new patients.' It just became a real struggle to even try to find a provider. I felt like my kids were just completely crashing while I was trying to muddle through paperwork," one parent told me.

The worry is *unrelenting* when a child has a life-threatening disease. As members of the Church, we must be on the lookout for those within our congregations and communities who are coping with these exhausting demands. From bishops and Relief Society presidents to quorum, Primary, youth, and Sunday School leaders, as well as friends and neighbors, there is much that the watchcare and ministering of a Latter-day Saint ward can do to aid families fighting this multifront war.

Isabela says she never felt abandoned by God, but she did feel very distant from Him. In moments of clarity, she remembers hoping Heavenly Father knew she was working on things. She recognized that the usual Sunday School answers—say your prayers, read your scriptures, go to church—might not "fix" her, but that didn't mean she was unrighteous or had sinned. "Mormons are doers," she says. "We are fixers, and there is a sense that we are supposed to be moving towards perfection and godliness. But depression just does not . . . I think depression prevents you from being able to do a lot of the things that others do."

Isabela is on the other side of the darkness; her illness is managed for the time being. She is a beautiful, compassionate, and newly married young woman with increased empathy for others who suffer. She was able to finish college and get a good job. Her illness has very little impact on her life today. Isabela wants people to know that depression doesn't define you and that you're still a beloved child of God even if, for a time, you can't feel His love. She's learned a lot about the stigmas that surround mental illness and why it's so hard to help someone who is suffering from depression. "Members of the Church like to check boxes," Isabela says. "We [pay] tithing and do our visiting teaching and check the box that says 'I paid my fast offerings and I helped clean the church on Saturday and I went to institute and I gave a ride to the young woman in need. . . . I cooked a meal for someone who had a baby.' It's hard to check a box for depression. It's hard to figure out what you need to do to check a box, to help someone with depression, partly because everyone's situation is so different and partly because it's kind of scary and unknown."

JEFF: TELLING THE TEAM

Jeff aspired to play baseball and football with his high-school team. Those dreams seemed to be dashed just before his freshman year when he was diagnosed with schizoaffective disorder. The disorder is a combination of bipolar symptoms (depression and mania) and schizophrenia. It took eighteen months of hospitalization and studying at a specialized school for Jeff to be well again.

With the proper medication, supervised nutrition and fitness routines, and a lot of support from family and friends, Jeff returned to a mainstream high school, where he found a place keeping statistics on the baseball team and a position as lineman on the football team. More remarkable, however, was Jeff's desire to tell his team about his condition. With encouragement from his coaches and parents, Jeff stood before more than fifty of his teammates and read a paper he had written about his experience, including this excerpt:

"Everyone might not land in the hospital with a mental breakdown like I did, but everyone struggles emotionally or mentally from time to time. Everyone might not need to go to a specialized school, but everyone is faced with challenges in class that can sometimes be overwhelming. I used to be afraid that if I mentioned I was having any trouble, I'd have to go back to the hospital. That's the last thing I'd want. But now I realize that it's important to ask for help before things get out of control. That's the difference between mental health and illness."

Today, Jeff is a high-school graduate and is studying at a university not far from his home. He continues to take medication and receive care for his mental illness. But it hasn't stopped him from living and loving life. He wants other teens who suffer to know "you can still reach very high in what you want to do and what you want to become. Keep your confidence up and stay optimistic," Jeff says. "Just keep going. Plow through adversity. You can eventually get to a point where you want to be. For me, for example, I just finished my freshman year of college studying computer science. . . . Everyone out there—I just want to tell them that no matter how tough your adversity is, keep plowing through, and never give up. And always ask for help. Sometimes that's the hardest part."

A MIRACLE: CECE'S STORY

Remember Cece, the young woman who rang my doorbell? When I spoke to her not long ago, she likened her experience of depression to standing on the shoreline of Utah Lake, watching a storm blow down the valley. All of a sudden, she said, "you're stuck in the middle of Utah Lake, and no matter where you step you can't get anywhere, you just start sinking, and there's rain and clouds everywhere. It feels like you're stuck in this mass of misery. You feel like you're going nowhere in life and you feel like you can't get out of it . . . like you can't move. It's the worst feeling I have ever felt in my life."

I asked Cece to tell me the story of the morning we'd shared so I could hear it from her perspective. In no small way, it's the story of a miracle, certainly of a life-changing—perhaps a lifesaving—gift of grace.

CECE: "I think it was January 2013. I was in a really, really dark place. It was so bad. I remember my mom kept coming into my room and saying, 'Come on, you need to get out of bed.' I had been in bed at that point for three days. At the time, I thought she was just angry, but looking back on it, the amount of worry in her face is astounding to me.

"I felt this rush of complete rage and complete defeat. I got up out of bed, put on some sweats, put on some shoes, and stormed out into the cold and started walking. My house was close to an interstate bridge at that point, and I was so low I thought, 'What if I went there and just jumped off? What if I just went and ended this whole thing right here, right now?'

"It was freezing, and there were cars passing by. I wasn't even thinking, I was just crying and shaking, and I thought, 'You know what? This is it. This is like—it.' I was at a place where I was accepting the fact that I was going to kill myself, that I was going to die, when something happened. I felt something on my shoulder. It felt like an arm. I heard a voice in my head saying, 'Turn around and go to Jane's house.' I ignored it; I blatantly ignored it for a good two or three minutes and kept walking. I thought, 'That's stupid. Why should I go see Jane? She's probably not home; she's probably busy.' I kept going. And then I literally felt someone turn me around and send me towards your house.

"I remember when I saw your car in the driveway I felt this rush of relief flowing through my body. I had stopped crying for a little bit as I was walking up your street. At that point, I realized that there was a little bit of hope, because Heavenly Father had guided me to someone who would help me, to someone who would be able to aid me in getting help and recovering. I remember feeling so grateful for the guidance that the Holy Ghost gives us when you opened your door and gave me a hug and told me to come in. All of those feelings of despair and loss and complete insecurity and loss of hope and faith: they were gone. I felt like I had a chance to start over. I felt like I had stepped out of a shower or something. I felt clean and I felt better. Because I had gotten so low that I finally let everything go and let Heavenly Father take care of things, that's when I knew that everything was going to be okay."

JANE: "I remember we were sitting on the couch when you told me how you were feeling and how you wanted to jump off the bridge. I said, 'We have to go get help right now.' I walked you downstairs, and we got in the car. I drove you to the emergency room, and we sat in the waiting room until your mom came."

CECE: "Yes, and as strange as it sounds, looking back on that day and those days I spent in the hospital and in therapy, they give me hope for the future. Because when you're so low that you're pushing yourself towards death, you cherish life a little bit more looking back on it. It's made me realize that helping other people is what Heavenly Father sent us to do. He has put us on this earth not only to fulfill our own missions and fulfill what He wants for us, but also to be physical angels to other people. I've seen that in my own life as I've progressed and recovered. I've been able to see not only how others have blessed my life, but how I've been able to help other people because of my experiences.

"Over time, I've found that I've learned how to bring people closer and how to make people feel included and help them feel safe. Because of my experiences, because I know what it feels like, I've been able to make sure they know that people are there for them."

JANE: "Why do you think there's so much misunderstanding, embarrassment, and often even shame attached to depression, anxiety, and mental illness?"

CECE: "Do you mean in general, or within people in the Church?"

JANE: "I think within the Church, specifically."

CECE: "I think there's a lot of shame attached to mental illness because people who are born into a covenant or even converts think that they're not supposed to have any problems. I feel like we are sent to earth to try to be like Christ. Sometimes members of the Church don't take into account that having a mental illness is not your fault. Sometimes it's just a side effect of life, but it doesn't mean you can't progress in trying to be like Christ. It doesn't mean that you can't recover, either."

When I asked Cece if her mental illness had affected her testimony, her relationship with God, and how she feels His Spirit, she said that it had at first. Like Claire, she felt a sense of betrayal—she couldn't understand why she had to endure such trials. She refused to go to church for a time and skipped her morning and evening prayers.

She didn't read her scriptures and would sleep through seminary or not attend at all. "That was in the beginning. After I started to get help, to get treatment, I started to lean on the gospel. I've learned that it really has strengthened my testimony, because in my deepest, darkest times, even after what has happened, turning to prayer or to pondering and reading conference talks brings me so much comfort. It brings me comfort because it helps me to know that I am not alone. Christ died for our sins . . . and it amazes me . . . He felt the pain that I was feeling.

"There are still days," she continues, "when I deal with hard things, especially as winter is coming around. But I've learned that it strengthens my testimony, because sometimes we can't rely on the natural man, on our own feelings and instincts. Sometimes we have to turn to Heavenly Father because He knows everything. He knows every single person on this earth inside out, and He knows how to help us. When we rely on His understanding and when we put our faith in Him and we let Him do the work and we follow what He needs us to do, then that's when we realize it's going to be okay."

I don't know if I've ever heard any deeper wisdom than that. Listening to Cece's testimony, I am so grateful that she came to my door that cold morning—for her sake, for my sake, and for all of us.

CHAPTER 6

CALLED TO SERVE, CALLED TO STRUGGLE: MISSIONARIES AND DEPRESSION

*Behold, the Lord requireth the heart and a willing
mind; and the willing and obedient shall eat the
good of the land of Zion in these last days.*

—DOCTRINE AND COVENANTS 64:34

I want you to find a way to make every missionary successful."
Those were the last words President Henry B. Eyring said to John
Robison and his wife, Joan, after calling John to be president of
the Texas Lubbock Mission. President Robison took those words seriously, especially when it came to elders and sisters in his mission who
suffered with clinical depression and anxiety.

Serving a mission is no easy feat. Latter-day Saint missionaries
don't choose where they are sent or the companions they must stay
"within sight and hearing of" for nearly every minute of every day
for up to two years. They pay their own expenses, and their working
day—seven days a week—lasts from 6:30 in the morning until 9:00
at night, with lights out at 10:30 (although the Church has recently
announced that schedules will become more flexible to better reflect
local cultures).

According to the *Missionary Handbook*, missionaries are "expected to devote all [their] time and attention to serving the Lord,

leaving behind all other personal affairs." They are allowed a letter or email message home each week (on preparation day only) and two telephone calls home per year. Never mind dating—even being alone with a member of the opposite sex is strictly forbidden, as are television, movies, and use of the Internet for anything but Church activities and authorized emails. Music listening is restricted to that which "invite[s] the Spirit, help[s] you focus on the work, and direct[s] your thoughts and feelings to the Savior." Headphones are not permitted, as they "isolate you from your companion."

Those are just the rules. The work itself can be tedious and discouraging. "Missions are very hard and quite different than most missionaries have a perception of before they leave," says Kevin Calderwood, former president of the New York New York South Mission. "Missionaries come out after hearing returned missionaries talk about the best of their missions, their greatest experiences, and rarely do they talk about the tough, difficult experiences, and so most young members of the Church have this perception of a mission just being a spiritual high, and they're going to be Ammon the day they enter the mission field, and everyone's going to run to the font when they start the testifying. They hear stories of the Book of Mormon, and stories from returned missionaries, and then they get out into the field, and people start rejecting them. They've got to get up at 6:30 and study and stay focused, and it's hard, and they're thinking for themselves, and they're lonely, and sometimes they're struggling."

Being a missionary is also an incredible rite of passage—rightly a source of tremendous pride for missionaries and their families. But as spiritually fulfilling and life changing as a mission can be, the days of hard work and making oneself vulnerable to frequent rejection and disappointment can be crushingly dispiriting. Being a missionary is simply one of the hardest things that anyone can do. The timing of missionary service requires many to set aside schooling and jobs at a time in their lives when their brains are still growing rapidly; researchers have determined that critical parts of the brain involved in decision making and emotional cognition are still developing well after legal adulthood is reached. In addition, missionaries are at precisely the age (eighteen to twenty-five) when the symptoms of many kinds of mental illness begin to present. Some missionaries (or their parents) may believe that the hardships of life in the field will toughen them (or their children) up. For some, that's exactly what happens. For many others, the opposite occurs.

FINDING SUCCESS IN THE FIELD: PRESIDENT JOHN ROBISON'S STEWARDSHIP

During his three years as a mission president in Texas, President John Robison gained a reputation as someone who was eager to help those with depression and anxiety. He graciously spoke with me about the struggles missionaries with depression face and how parents, leaders, and other missionaries can best support these young people, whether they stay in the mission field or return home.

"When the manifestation of mental illness at any level becomes apparent to a mission president," Robison says, "then at that point in time, your priority is to help this young man or young woman. Not necessarily try to cure them, because that's a long process, but to do everything we can at that point in time to forget about the baptisms and forget about companionship study and individual study and make your focus this young person. The first question has to be, 'What can I do to help them get through this?' If it means keeping them in the mission field, 'What's it going to take for me to keep them in the mission field so that they conclude feeling an element of success that they finished and not worry about how productive they are?'"

For Robison, that meant to first find a compassionate companion and to then place the pair in an area where the members and the bishop were able to reach out to them. His goal: "To surround them with people that would just love them."

Then Robison would sit down and talk honestly with the missionary about how he or she was feeling. When necessary, he enlisted doctors and counselors to get the elders and sisters needed medication and therapy. He considered each missionary on a case-by-case basis. Elder Morris,* for example, came to Robison's mission with a history of depression. He'd already gone home from the MTC to manage an episode of the illness. While at home, Morris had been called as a Church Service Missionary, received the therapy and medication he needed, and prepared to return to the field. The Missionary Department asked President Robison if he would take Elder Morris in his mission rather than sending him to the one to which he'd originally been assigned. Robison did so enthusiastically.

"I sat him down when he came, and I said, 'Look, I want to do everything we can to help you.' We had a rule at that time that the missionaries couldn't drink caffeinated drinks. . . .

"[Elder Morris] said to me, 'I just need a Diet Coke every so often.' I said, 'Then you can have a Diet Coke.' He goes, 'Seriously?' I said, 'Absolutely.' I said, 'You buy it on your P day. You put it in your apartment. I'll tell your companion it's okay. . . . If you want a Diet Coke, have a Diet Coke.' . . .

"I cut him a little bit of slack, and I didn't make a big deal about it, like I didn't announce it or whatever, but I just tried to modify some of the rigidity that you have to have within the mission field. I modified that for him, and I did it for several others. You know what? It wasn't so much that he could drink a Diet Coke. It was like the pressure was off that he couldn't drink a Diet Coke. . . . It just

*Name has been changed.

97

took away such a minor thing, but for a kid who's going through difficult issues, that's a big deal."

Robison also spoke with the Missionary Department at Church headquarters, Elder Morris, and his parents, and arranged permission for Morris to be released after eighteen months in the field rather than twenty-four. Robison explained that Morris's time as a Church Service Missionary could count toward time in the field, and his request was approved. At eighteen months, Elder Morris was honorably released and able to go home feeling successful, a huge victory for someone battling depression. "He finished with his head held high," Robison said. Today Morris is married and a father. Robison had fulfilled President Eyring's counsel "to make every missionary successful."

Sister Jones is another of President Robison's missionaries. Though she experienced symptoms of anxiety and depression during her childhood and teen years, Sister Jones had never identified them as such or been diagnosed. But after three weeks at the Missionary Training Center, she began to have trouble sleeping and lost her appetite. "I kept thinking that if I could shake the physical symptoms, my problems would go away," she told me. "It was really hard because I would receive blessings saying that I'd be able to sleep, but I didn't sleep. Priesthood leaders would tell me to have more faith, and that got me in a downward spiral because I thought it was on me. I thought it was because I wasn't obedient enough. I thought it was because I wasn't working hard enough. I just started obsessing over the rules, thinking, 'It's my fault that this is happening to me.'"

Eventually Sister Jones departed for her mission in Peru. After four weeks in the country, she found herself at an all-time low. "I felt like a zombie," she said. "I would just follow my companion around like a dog. I was super emotional. I felt like I looked different. I had suicidal ideation. I didn't have a plan to hurt myself, but I would think, 'Look at that bus coming out. I want that bus to hit me.'

Those are scary thoughts, but I was so low. I thought that I was failing, that I was letting everyone down—my family, my mission, and,
most importantly, I felt like I was letting my Savior down. That's why
it was so hard for me to understand. I would just read and pray and
pray. I wanted to serve and I couldn't. Not physically, emotionally, or
spiritually. I was just a mess."

Eventually, the mission doctors decided that it would be best for
Sister Jones to return home. She miraculously endured forty-eight
hours of solo travel with little understanding of the language and no
sleep. Though her parents and stake president were supportive, her return was difficult. The well-laid plans of adolescence had been flipped
upside down. She missed the happy, healthy young woman that she'd
once been. Additionally, there was the awkwardness she felt when she
explained her situation to ward members and acquaintances. "I'd tell
them, 'I was really sick,'" she recalled, "and immediately they would
ask, 'Oh, did you get a parasite?' Then I'd say, 'You know, I'm suffering from anxiety and depression.' And then they wouldn't know what
to say. It wasn't something that was tangible, and if they hadn't gone
through it themselves, they didn't think it was real. They'd assume I
was homesick or that I just couldn't hack it."

Throughout her difficulties, Sister Jones continued praying,
though she uncharacteristically struggled to feel the Spirit. After
counseling with her father and other trusted leaders, she decided
to return to the mission field. Instead of Peru, she was assigned to
President Robison's mission in Lubbock, Texas. There she was
strengthened by Joan Robison, President Robison's wife, who had experienced postpartum depression and was extremely understanding
and supportive. There was also, of course, President Robison, with his
compassionate plan for missionaries with depression.

"There were times when I was worried because I wasn't feeling
the Spirit, or I didn't feel like I was on my A-game, that the Lord

couldn't use me," Sister Jones admitted. "But then when I would tell people about some of my struggles, they would say, 'I wouldn't have known,' or, 'That lesson you gave, the Spirit really touched me.' Even though I wasn't necessarily feeling it myself, if I could testify of a truth, the Spirit could work with that. Of course I made mistakes and I wasn't the best missionary, but it was good to know that the Lord can still use you if you are not 100 percent."

Sister Jones began looking for other ways that she could recognize the Holy Ghost speaking to her. "I was so numb. I couldn't feel anything. Mental illness is a physiological problem, so if you're used to feeling the Spirit through feelings, it's really hard. I had to learn to find the Spirit in other ways.

"One time," she says, "I was sitting with my companion, but I wasn't really there mentally. I felt the sun beating down on me and I just felt warm. I felt like that was Heavenly Father saying, 'I'm still here. I still love you.'"

Sister Jones emerged from the abyss of her disease with rare insights and miraculous grace. "All the Lord requires of you is your best, and your best can change," she explained. "Sometimes my best is getting out of bed. That was my best for that day. Sometimes I was doing really well, and I was able to do all the things that a missionary's supposed to do. I had to learn how to be okay with that. I still struggle with that, even today. The Lord just requires your best, and your best changes. And that is okay."

President Robison and his wife were angels, Sister Jones says. As with Elder Morris, Robison adjusted the rules at times to help Sister Jones. Some days she might be dropped off at the mission home and spend time with Sister Robison, who counseled her and cheered her up while Sister Jones's companion worked with another set of sisters for the day. "She got it, meaning she had been through it. She just loved me and was there for me. She was one of those people I could be around and feel good. I still had my struggles in Texas, but I learned so many things, and this is something I give her," Sister Jones says of Sister Robison. It was little comforts like this and the permission to go home early some nights for additional rest that helped Sister Jones stay as healthy as possible until she completed her mission.

FINDING MIRACLES: SISTER THRALL'S STORY

Sister Thrall's story is not unlike Sister Jones's, but it took place on the other side of the world. Sister Thrall was thrilled with her call to the Russia Moscow Mission and departed full of hope and enthusiasm. That hope, however, was short lived. "I remember getting to the MTC and being so ready to take on the whole world," she says. "I was there for twelve weeks. I think it was around week nine or ten when I felt it . . . that dark heaviness. I was so surprised and somewhat devastated. I received a lot of counsel and a few priesthood blessings, and I left for Russia. The first few weeks seemed to be free of the darkness in some ways, but then it came back, and I found that I was crying all of the time. I based a lot of my progress, or lack thereof, on how frequently I cried. But even at that point, I don't think I called it depression. I avoided the word like a plague."

For months, Sister Thrall stuck it out, but not without a lot of very dark moments. She heartbreakingly recalls a number of "firsts" that occurred during the seven months she tried to dodge the word *depression*: "My mission was the catalyst for a lot of firsts. It was the first time that I engaged in self-harm, just small things like poking myself with needles or scratching myself or banging my head against the wall. It was the first time that I have actually been mad at God. I was so angry with Him, and I told Him so. This turned out to be very good for our relationship in the end, but it was almost a source of shame at the time. It was also the first time I had thoughts of suicide. That scared me. More than anything else that happened my whole mission, it scared me into action. I told my companion and I got help."

She refers to the day before she told her companion as the worst day of her life. It was a day, however, that proved fruitful because it drove her to ask for help and stop fighting the battle alone. The medication she was prescribed wasn't a cure-all, but Sister Thrall thinks it's unlikely that she could have finished her mission without it. She also could not have persevered without a mission president who was compassionate and understanding. Small adjustments and frequent check-ins made a huge difference and are great examples of what mission presidents can do to help a missionary who wants to serve—and who, with counseling and medication, has the capacity to do so. I love how Sister Thrall described the support she received:

"My mission president was very understanding. He let me call home a few times to talk with my mom. My mother kept me on my mission with her faith in me and her love and her gentle encouragement. I know I would have come home early, like into my third transfer early, if my mission president had not let me speak to her.

"There were also two times on my mission when I spent a week with a senior missionary couple. Once after I called my mom the first time, during my third transfer, while the mission president arranged an emergency transfer. And once right after the darkest day on my mission. The wisdom, the love, the comfort of those two couples gave me the refreshment and rejuvenation that I needed to keep going. I really needed a break! It was so hard, and I just needed a few days when it was okay for me to rest and be with strong couples who were not burdened by the schedule and rejection of missionary work like I was. Their responsibilities were different, and I was thankful for that.

"At the darkest times in my mission I was blessed with very strong and supportive companions. They saw me cry a lot! And they loved me through it all! They were amazing women, and I'm so thankful for their support. I was honest with them, and they were patient with me."

Sister Thrall learned coping skills on her mission that continue to help her as she battles recurring bouts of depression. She learned to go to others for help and came to recognize that God felt her pain, even when she couldn't describe it herself. She adopted a wonderful habit that sustained some optimism during long days spent searching for investigators and alternating between teaching moments and rejection. "I would pick up coins off the ground," she says. "Everywhere I went, I looked for them. At the end of the day I had to say a miracle that happened for every coin. I still do that today. It really helped me to focus on the little things that could easily be overlooked but in reality were huge signs that God loved me."

THE OTHER SIDE OF THE COIN: JESSI'S EXPERIENCE

More than twelve years ago, Jessi came home early from her mission feeling broken. "I felt shut out," she says. A few people judged her for coming home early. One leader's reaction—and later interaction with her—was outright unkind. Her mother had—and sometimes still has—a difficult time understanding the feelings that surround depression and anxiety. Jessi herself worried at first that her "failure" meant "nobody would want to marry me." For months after returning home, she felt "abandoned by God"; going to church, she says, was "torture." Even today, as a married mother of two young children, her feelings are still raw when she talks about her mission.

A thread of residual anger runs like a current through her mind when she looks back. She can't help but wonder what the outcome might have been with a different mission president, one who was more supportive and willing to accommodate her needs. Jessi worries about the young men and women of today who come home with the same crippling feelings she did. She wants these challenges "to be recognized, acknowledged, and discussed."

To those missionaries who "come home and are just confused and in pain, and have those oozing wounds," Jessi says: "It's okay. It's okay to be a mess. And it's okay that you dread church. And it's okay that you don't feel like anybody can relate to you. And it's okay if every time somebody mentions missionary work you just want to run out of the room and curl up in a ball and cry. And it's okay if you can't feed the missionaries because it's too painful."

These are not atypical manifestations of depression. In the case of early returned missionaries, the challenges associated with their return may aggravate their depression, and the depression may, in turn, aggravate unnecessarily negative feelings about their missionary experience and themselves. Therapy, medication, time, and a good support system can help depressed individuals resolve these feelings. Even those missionaries with mission presidents or other leaders who aren't as supportive as those mentioned in this chapter can heal eventually. Jessi wants others like her to know it's okay to "live in a place of pain" for a time. And, "if the pain doesn't go away, that doesn't mean that you're not doing your best."

SELF-DISCIPLINE VS. SELF-DENIAL

Dr. Leslie Feinauer is a marriage and family therapist and former professor of marriage and family therapy at BYU. She currently serves as a mental-health adviser in Europe, helping young elders and sisters with depression and other mental illnesses. Dr. Feinauer explains a phenomenon in which members of our Church—and missionaries in particular—turn the gospel into a "hair shirt." Woven from goat hair, hair shirts were designed in biblical times to be scratchy and uncomfortable. Some Catholic ascetics wore them to show the Lord how much they loved Him. Still others, called flagellants, whipped themselves. These practices—called "self-mortification"—have no official place in our Church, but missionaries can be susceptible to that kind of thinking. On a mission, desires that were once normal for teenagers—to want to sleep late, watch movies, hang out with friends, date, or wear jeans and other casual clothes—are suddenly inappropriate and can feel unrighteous. In this environment of self-denial, young missionaries can wrongly believe that the Lord will not love them unless they are suffering. Too much perfectionism and self-judgment can lead to the same mistaken conclusion—that the Lord doesn't want us to be happy or to have things that we enjoy. In the hell of depression, thoughts of that kind can lead to self-harm and even suicide.

Dr. Feinauer worked to help missionaries avoid this thinking. She told me how she helped one sister, who was struggling with severe depression and anxiety, understand this and the difference between self-discipline and excessive self-denial. One day, Dr. Feinauer asked this young sister what she would do that day if she could do anything she wanted. The sister replied that she'd like to walk down to the banks of a lovely river that flowed through their town. When Dr. Feinauer suggested she do just that, the sister refused. "I can't," she said. "There are hardly any people down there and I have to talk to 700 people today."

Dr. Feinauer told her, "Well then, you're going to do an experiment, and you're only going to do this because I'm asking. You're going to break the rule that you have in your head and you're going to go down to the river. You can talk to everybody on the way, but you're going to walk down to the river and back."

The sister took some convincing, but she finally agreed to go, provided that Dr. Feinauer took the blame if something bad happened. "You have to carry the guilt for this," the sister said. Dr. Feinauer agreed, and the sister and her companion set off for the river.

Every five minutes the sister told her companion that they couldn't do this. "I have to go back," she said. "But you promised you would do this," her companion replied. "We're just going to go down to the river, and then we can come right back."

When they were three-fourths of the way there, her companion suddenly stopped in her tracks. "Remember that woman we met two weeks ago that we haven't been able to find?" she said excitedly. "That's her house! I just saw her walk by the window." They went and knocked on her door, and the woman invited them in, saying that she'd hoped to see them again but didn't know how to find them. They agreed to return and teach her after they'd been to the river.

"We talked later about that desire she had had to go down and walk by that wonderful river," Dr. Feinauer concluded. "That was the Spirit. She was having a hard time hearing it because it was also a desire she had. She thought the Spirit would only make her do hard things that she didn't want to do. She thought that God only pushes us to do things that we don't want to do that are righteous, and that He would never tell us to do something that we enjoyed."

After that, things began to change for this sister. As she and her companion returned to the river again and again to teach their new friend, she increasingly felt God's love and sensed that He was a kind, sensitive parent. She saw that her desire for beauty was good and righteous and that the Lord could use that desire for His work. This is how grace happens—miraculously and unexpectedly.

PHYSICAL LABOR, SERVICE, AND SLEEP: LESSONS FROM SUPERSTORM SANDY

Kevin Calderwood was serving as the mission president in the area when Superstorm Sandy slammed the northeast coast of the United States in 2012. He spoke with me about what happened when the missionaries under him exchanged their suits and skirts for work clothes and bright yellow vests and spent weeks helping Northeasterners clean up after the storm.

JANE: "When Superstorm Sandy hit, what happened in your mission as far as mental-health issues were concerned?"

PRESIDENT CALDERWOOD: "We had several missionaries going to counseling prior to Hurricane Sandy, or Superstorm Sandy, and when the storm hit, our goal was to first be safe ourselves, then go and serve others. We fanned out in the communities, first going to our members, but when the neighborhood saw us serving members, especially in the Belle Harbor Rockaway area, they just came over and pled with us for help.

"The missionaries felt needed, they could see that their service was extremely meaningful, and it was very fulfilling to them. They couldn't wait to get back the next day. They recognized that these people were their fellow men who were hurting, and that they had an opportunity to go in and to help them. During that four-month period, where we were working almost every day in the homes and basements of the people whose homes were flooded, our mental-health issues were few to none. The counseling went down because missionaries were focused on other people, not worried about themselves, and they were feeling very fulfilled in their service. They could see that it was worthwhile and meaningful, and so the combination of that fulfillment helped them emotionally, and then specifically, they were out doing rigorous work. It just declined dramatically during that four-month period."

JANE: "There's a difference between dysthymia, or serious depressive disorder, and someone who's homesick, right?"

PRESIDENT CALDERWOOD: "A dramatic difference."

JANE: "Can you speak to that a little bit? How did that play into the equation?"

PRESIDENT CALDERWOOD: "It did. All of us get blue, all of us get homesick, and some people are taught that you're not supposed to feel. We tell our missionaries go ahead and feel. Feel it all. We're here on this earth to feel all of these emotions, but then get over them and move forward. Those that just have the blues, those that are kind of homesick or struggling or not wanting to work, they buckle up and they get to work.

"There are some missionaries—we had several of them—though, that had a dramatic illness. It was deep depression. . . . That group of missionaries was very different. You had to be very careful with them, but I'll tell you, even that group of missionaries was much healthier during this time of selfless service and giving back, because the community down there needed so much help. It helped them forget about their own concerns, and they were even more healthy. They still needed their medication, it's like any other illness, but it seemed to taper off. Even missionaries, in my opinion, who had severe illness, when their mind was somewhere else, and when they were happy and fulfilled, even that illness got better."

JANE: "Obviously, it was selfless service. Was it also the heavy, physical labor? Was that part of it?"

PRESIDENT CALDERWOOD: "It was a big part of it. They were getting up, they were tired, they were working . . . carrying couches, and furnaces, and tables, and belongings, and boxes. They were working very hard. At the end of the day, they were covered in mud from head to toe, just exhausted. Therefore, they got a good night's sleep. I'll tell you, sleep is a wonderful thing for all of it, homesickness or an illness. So, the hard labor, good sleep, as well as the focus outside of themselves . . . it really helped the emotional and physical state of the missionaries."

Many stories of missionaries with mental-health issues result in the hoped-for outcome, as we have seen, but, as President Robison says, "Mental illness isn't one size fits all." He remembers two missionaries with depression whom he couldn't help. They returned home despite his best efforts. In fact, for a significant number of depression-challenged missionaries, prayer, counseling, and medicine are inadequate. One report from 2014 states that 6 percent of the 82,000 plus missionaries in the field don't complete their full term of service for health reasons—and today the number is reported to be even higher.

EXPERIENCES OF EARLY-RETURNED MISSIONARIES

Dr. Kris Doty-Yells, former chair of the Behavioral Science Department at Utah Valley University, led a major 2015 study on returned missionaries. She found that only 11 percent of the survey sample came home early because they'd broken a rule or committed some serious indiscretion. Thirty-four percent of them had a physical illness or injury, while 36 percent had mental-health concerns.

What is the Church's attitude toward that substantial majority of early returnees whose missions were cut short by illness? For the most part, it is one of compassion and understanding. In a video posted on his Facebook page prior to a Face-to-Face event in 2016, Elder Jeffrey R. Holland responded movingly to a question posed by a young missionary who had returned after just four months in the field. "It's really difficult," the missionary had written, "not to feel like a failure. I'm not even sure if it was my fault. What do I do? How can I look at my short mission the way that I should?"

While Elder Holland emphasized that his answer was personal and not necessarily the law and gospel for the Church, he spoke with deep emotion, directly from his heart. "Obviously," he said, "we want everyone to have a full and complete mission. We're anxious that no one succumb to homesickness or battle fatigue and truncate their mission. . . .

But listen . . . there are reasons that people can't serve a mission. There are reasons that people can't go on a mission in the first place. We know that. We understand that. And in this particular reference, the reason was a mental health issue. I love the honesty of that, the candor of that. And I certainly recognize the legitimacy of that. And there would be some in that category who would not be able to serve a mission at all.

"So I say commendation to you, and the love of the Lord to you, and the blessings of the Church to you for trying to go, for wanting to go, and for the fact that you successfully served for four months. It obviously wasn't a full term, but it was missionary service. It was honest. You were loyally participating and testifying. And I want you to take credit for that. I want you to take the appropriate dignity that you deserve from that and to know that the Lord loves you and the Church loves you for serving. . . .

"I don't want you to apologize for coming home. When someone asks you if you've served a mission, you say yes. You do not need to follow that up with, 'But it was only four months.' Just forget that part and say yes, you served a mission and be proud of the time that you spent."

While the Church itself does not attach stigma to a mission cut short due to illness, many missionaries do—and so do their parents and other members of the Church. Dr. Doty-Yells—who is the mother of two early returnees (both subsequently went back out in the field only to come home early again)—found that 73 percent of the participants in her survey suffered from feelings of failure and that two-thirds felt discomfort in social settings due to their early releases. Fewer than half (46 percent) felt confident stating "I'm a returned missionary," and 44 percent felt uncomfortable answering questions about their missions. Forty percent felt pressured to go back out, 37 percent reported adverse effects on their dating lives, and only 37 percent said they felt connected to those who completed their missions successfully. Dr. Doty-Yells's study is filled with accounts of shaming—by parents, ward members, and coworkers:

"I went back to Provo and started working at [a restaurant] again. It is where I worked before. It is not that people were really looking down on me a lot—but there were a lot of jokes going back and forth. I remember my supervisor was telling me to finish cleaning the steamers and I was like, 'Yeah, I will finish them.' And he said, 'Really? Just like you finished your mission?'"

"The mission president phoned my stake president and I got to call my parents. I called my mom and she just started crying. I told my dad and he tells me that he has failed me as a father. I won't be able to come home. There won't be a bed for me there."

"I think the hardest thing is people's expectations. I felt like I wasn't meeting their expectations, so I was being treated differently. I never really felt accepted [or] like people understood the whole situation."

As people who are under covenant to share the burdens of others, it seems unconscionable that we would instead, in any way, add to those burdens through stigmatization and uncharitable judgments. All of us have the opportunity to either help or hamper early-returned missionaries in resuming their lives while simultaneously trying to leap a mental-health hurdle or any other challenge. I think of this passage from the Apostle Paul's epistle to the Romans:

"For it is written, As I live, saith the Lord, every knee shall bow to me, and every tongue shall confess to God. So then every one of us shall give account of himself to God. Let us not therefore judge one another any more: but judge this rather, that no man put a stumblingblock or an occasion to fall in his brother's way" (Romans 14:11–13).

Jenifer and I communicated via email about her missionary experience and the stigma that followed her early return. Depression struck from the blue, like a boulder rolling down a hill. "Within a period of two weeks," she wrote, "I [was] delusional, hospitalized without my mission companion, sent home on medical leave, [and] released from my missionary service." The experience was traumatizing. She wrote that when she initially returned home, she felt:

"This shouldn't be happening to me—not someone who had a sure witness that God approved of my decision to serve a mission. I felt awkward when I'd run into someone who knew that I had come home early from my mission. When my brothers' friends came over, I discreetly wandered into a different room in the house. Their judgments didn't need to be spoken; I could hear the chastisement loudly in my mind. I sent a long letter of gratitude to my mission president for his help and tried to express my hope that my experience may help some future missionary who suffered with mental illness. I never received a response. My compassionate mission companion sent me some photographs of us at the Statue of Liberty and at an investigator's home. She included a sincere letter, reminding me of our remarkable week before my hospitalization. Other than these two interactions, I never heard from anyone. Not only did I feel culturally compelled to hide my diagnosis and treatment, but it seemed to me that some Church leaders and my mission friends thought I should too."

As Jenifer's story attests, not every mission president will be as experienced, tolerant, and sensitive as some of those described in this chapter. And individual Church members fall on a wide spectrum ranging from very charitable and kind to thoughtless and even highly judgmental. Fortunately, the Church itself is making conscious efforts to better address depression and anxiety in missionaries. Many leaders, like Elder Holland and an increasing number of mission presidents, bishops, and stake presidents, are helping to bring the problem into the light. I hope this book will add to their efforts. We need to keep at it!

WHAT CAN WE DO?

Like the elders and sisters they lead, mission presidents aren't im-
mune to the challenges of mental illness. Jim MacArthur, a psychologist, former director of the BYU Counseling Center, and a former
mission president, shared a particularly moving experience about his
own struggle with depression while serving in South America. "I was
sixty-five when I was called," he told me. "I hadn't spoken Spanish in
forty-six years.

"I brought a history of mild depression and anxiety with me into
the mission field. There is a long history of it in our family for various
reasons. It was important to me to acknowledge this tendency in myself under the immense pressure of my new calling.

"When I first got to Chile, I sat on my bed and cried because
I thought I was going to fail. I was so overwhelmed. I was so depressed. I battled my way through it for a period of time and then
realized medication could help me, along with my own efforts. Then
I decided to share my journey with missionaries at appropriate times,
when I saw it would help them to know we were fellow travelers.
I wanted them to understand you can wrestle with these things and
still faithfully serve the Lord.

"Missionaries would say to me, 'I just feel so hopeless and helpless.' I'd say to them, 'Put your hands across the desk. You take my
hand; I'll take your hands. You and I have stepped onto this same
path at the same time today, and we are going to go a distance together. You just hold on to my hand. I'm going to go that journey
with you and I'll understand it as best I can.'"

President Steven H. Stewart recalled apostolic counsel he received
during his training. "When I was called to be a mission president, we
went down to the MTC for the New Mission Presidents' Seminar.
I remember hearing Elder Oaks talk about mental illness and depression and anxiety among missionaries, and he used a comparison to

diabetes, as I recall. He said, 'You can't tell somebody to buck up if they've got a chemical imbalance, so don't look at it like they're not praying hard enough and they're not working hard enough, or that they can just convince themselves that they can do it. Look at it from a medical perspective.' That stuck with me."

Small flexibilities in the rules, expectations that can be adapted to the capabilities of a struggling missionary, and attention to the atmosphere of love and support required by a depression sufferer are all inspired choices by concerned mission presidents. President Stewart explained one of the techniques he employed to reduce pressure on individual missionaries. "For example, when we published a monthly newsletter, we would list the names of the converts in that newsletter, but we would not associate those converts with a specific companionship of missionaries. We would just put the names of the converts when they were baptized and confirmed. I wanted everybody to consider that those were our converts—the mission's converts."

President Kevin Calderwood said he also found that some missionaries suffered when they measured themselves only by their results. So he emphasized progress: "I saw missionaries go through this and it broke my heart. I spent a lot of time trying to tell them, 'No, you're great. You've got a lifetime and beyond to grow to where you need to be. Just Relax, with a capital 'R,' take it at a right pace, and grow.'"

An ecclesiastical leader who is educated and empathetic about depression is always a boon to one who suffers from it, but mission presidents can't go it alone.

What can we—friends, family, Church leaders, and congregation members—do to sustain missionaries who are struggling with mental illness? Support and wisdom are required long before the missionary is issued a mission call, and parents and spiritual leaders should be sensitive to the question of whether young people are fully prepared for the challenges they will face. Sometimes it can be tempting to try to just "get them on their mission" and hope that this will clear up their mental, emotional, or spiritual struggles. This can be a very risky approach. Instead, leaders and parents should treat each young person's situation individually. Being prepared for a mission is much more than being able to answer all the questions correctly.

Teaching young people basic stress-coping techniques (like deep breathing, keeping a journal, going for a walk, saying a prayer) can be extremely effective. If teenagers are already showing signs of mental illness before they leave, it's important that they be prepared and able to manage it. Things like having the discipline and responsibility to take their medications on time are essential for success as a missionary.

Missionaries who need to return home early are especially vulnerable, but parents and leaders can pave the way for them to have better homecomings. Here are a few suggestions compiled from the mission presidents, former missionaries, and mission doctors I've interviewed:

- Treat their homecoming like any other missionary's.
- Listen. Be understanding and nonjudgmental.
- Seek out counseling options and medical treatment when indicated.
- Be appropriately open with family and friends. Most of the stigma that early returnees experience results from misunderstanding; people assume that there has been a serious transgression. With the missionary's permission, clarify the reason for the return.
- Don't take the situation personally. This isn't your fault. Your child's illness is not a reflection on you. Be proud of your missionary for what they were able to accomplish during their service and support them in their recovery. They need love, not judgment.
- Don't pressure your child to return to the mission field. Treating emotional illnesses takes time, and your missionary may have

given enough service already. Seek counsel from your bishop, Church headquarters, and medical professionals.

When Melaney's son Max came home early from his mission several years ago, Melaney was determined not to let the stigma stick. Before he arrived, they had spoken with him on the phone and could sense the depth of his depression. He was so low he could barely speak. And when he did, his voice was slow and full of pain. Melaney made a decision right away: "I just made the judgment call to do a broadcast email to all of the friends and family that I thought would want to know this." With her permission, I share portions of the email below. It is a remarkable example of faith and love, and it proved to be exactly the right thing to do in Max's case.

> *Dear Friends,*
>
> *We wanted to let you each know that Max will be returning home today from his mission and will be receiving a medical missionary release.*
>
> *He is suffering from a deep depression that none of us, including mission leaders, knew about. He has already started receiving care in the field and will continue with that care here at home. The option of returning to the field is available to him at a later date, and, once he is feeling like himself again, we will address that. We also look forward to him continuing to have a rich experience in our ward in the short term.*
>
> *We ask for your prayers for him and are so thankful in advance for the loving concern we know you each feel. While this will be a challenge of a lifetime for him, we feel optimistic and grateful—for modern medical help and divine, spiritual healing. The Atonement of our Lord just keeps on giving. . . .*
>
> *While we fully respect Max's privacy, we also want you to know that our door is open—to visit, to discuss, to better*

understand. Please don't worry about how to interact with him or us—just go for it!

Max received an outpouring of love, especially from his stake president, who embraced him upon releasing him and served as an example for others in the stake and ward to follow. On Max's first Sunday back to church, a loving high councilor felt inspired to speak of his own early release from his mission. "[He] shared some of his experience and his gratitude for having served," Melaney said. "I had never known that about him, and here's Max, his first Sunday back, watching this faithful, wonderful, happy man, share that that was part of his life experience. . . . Here he is, standing to tell about it, without embarrassment, without stigma."

Because Max's family was so open, he didn't have to worry about stigma, only about getting better. That, of course, took time and some trial and error; he still requires treatment on occasion. Melaney reports that about six weeks after his return, Max gave a phenomenal homecoming talk in sacrament meeting. Melaney had worried that Max's experience would diminish his faith, especially because it's so difficult to feel the Spirit when depressed. But she learned that faith does not always equate to the ability to feel the Spirit. "I realize that you can decide that your faith is real, your conversion and your conviction to the gospel and the Restoration are real, even while you have periods when you're not feeling the Spirit," she says. "I'm not sure how we cultivate that among our depressed population, but it doesn't have to be a given that those times when they stop feeling the Spirit necessarily mean that they have to give up on their faith."

Leaders like Max's stake president and the thoughtful high council speaker can help struggling young missionaries feel valued, understood, and supported.

God's love is powerful—it shines through in each and every one of the interviews I've conducted for this book. Almost without exception, the missionaries I talked to told me that they'd emerged from their struggles with a deeper understanding of God's love, an enhanced gratitude for the Savior's Atonement and increased capacity to access its power, and a more charitable view toward others.

Over and over again, I heard people speak of their knowledge of a kind, loving, accepting Father. Carol, whose son Tim returned early with debilitating depression, talked about how her understanding of grace had changed since her son had been afflicted with this disease. It's easy to think of grace as "go 90 percent and the Lord will make up the rest" when you are active and healthy, fulfilling callings, attending meetings, and having spiritual experiences, she explained. But when people are brought to their knees by a disease, grace suddenly plays a whole new role. "Christ has done everything," she said to me. "He will be there for you even when you can't keep one commandment."

Carol described to me an image she created that comforted her and helped her relate to Tim while he battled depression and anxiety in the days after his early return and the months and years that followed. She pinned a picture of the Savior to a wall near her bed. In the picture, the Savior's arms are out, as if He is giving a blessing. She placed a picture of Tim under the Savior's arms. Each day, during prayer and meditation, she looked at this image and reminded herself that Tim was in the Savior's hands, that his path may not be the same as that of other missionaries or his peers generally, but his promises from the Savior are of equal grandeur.

As the scripture that opens this chapter reassures us, our willingness to serve the Lord is an offering that He honors and blesses, and a willing mind is acceptable to Him even if that mind is plagued by illness and our capacity to serve is limited. If the Lord finds such service honorable, so should we all.

CHAPTER 7

NOT JUST THE BABY BLUES: POSTPARTUM DEPRESSION

I am a woman of a sorrowful spirit: . . . out of the
abundance of my complaint and grief have I spoken.

—HANNAH, IN 1 SAMUEL 1:15–16

Motherhood is a tall order. President Russell M. Nelson has called it "the highest and noblest work in this life." And Sister Julie B. Beck, former Relief Society General President, said, "There is eternal influence and power in motherhood."

I believe these statements to be true. For me, being a righteous mother is the very embodiment of success. But I am only human and know too well how often I've fallen short of what I feel I should be. At the nadir of my depression, I walled myself off from my husband and my children; worse still, I was often angry at them for no reason. I didn't want to be—I knew it was wrong, but my guilt only made things worse. I know now that I was sick; I was no more to blame for not being able to meet all the demands of my high calling than if I had come down with pneumonia or had broken both my legs. But it didn't feel that way at the time. I can't imagine having those feelings while simultaneously recovering from childbirth and caring for a newborn.

FROM BABY BLUES TO CLINICAL ILLNESS

Tragically, for many new mothers, the sudden drop in estrogen and progesterone levels that comes with childbirth triggers just that: a clinical mood disorder that robs the new mother of joy and engulfs her in a cloud of anxiety, anger, and discontent. The symptoms of this disease—and a postpartum mood disorder *is* a disease, not a character defect, a product of wrong thinking, or a lack of will—can present immediately after birth or many months later. Some women feel fine until they wean their babies, and then shifting hormones bring on depression. The symptoms cover a spectrum that ranges from the persistent sadness and emotional volatility that are quaintly called the "baby blues," which usually dispel without intervention after a few weeks, to the overwhelming fatigue, uncontrollable crying, emotional withdrawal, severe panic attacks, insomnia, inability to concentrate or make decisions, and suicidal ideation that are the hallmarks of clinical depression. Very rarely, they tip into full-blown psychosis. This is what happened to Andrea Yates, the Texas mother who was diagnosed with postpartum psychosis after the birth of her fourth child, and who, after several suicide attempts, drowned her children after giving birth to the fifth.

According to the Centers for Disease Control, as many as one in five of the four million women who give birth in the United States each year will suffer from a postpartum mood disorder. Women with a history of depression are at greater risk, as are women who suffer from stressors such as lack of sufficient emotional support at home or in the community, low education, poverty, and abuse. Teenaged mothers face a higher risk, as do the mothers of babies who are admitted to neonatal intensive care units. By even the most conservative estimate, more women will develop postpartum mood disorders each year than are diagnosed with strokes (300,000 in the U.S.) or breast cancer (250,000). According to the website Postpartum Progress, there are more new cases of postpartum depression every year than tuberculosis, leukemia, multiple sclerosis, Parkinson's disease, Alzheimer's disease, and epilepsy combined (and among both men and women). Yet little is done to prepare expectant mothers for this possibility.

As Dr. Ruta Nonacs of Massachusetts General Hospital and Harvard Medical School notes: "All women receiving prenatal care are screened for diabetes, but how many pregnant and postpartum women are screened for depression? PPD is also more common than preterm labor, low birth weight, pre-eclampsia and high blood pressure; in other words, PPD is the most common complication associated with pregnancy and childbirth."

The many women I interviewed for this chapter prove Doctor Nonacs's point, and I wish there was space here to include all of their stories because each teaches a lesson of reliance—on friends, on family, and on herself—and faith. Each story also adds to the narrative of depression—a crucial narrative that, if shared, helps destroy the stigma surrounding the disease. These are just a few representative stories.

OPPOSITION IN ALL THINGS: THE EXPECTATIONS OF EXPECTING

We describe a pregnant woman as "expecting," by which we mean she is expecting a baby. But there's a complicated bundle of additional expectations that comes along with that, unique to each woman. Most are happy, or want to be. Anticipation is part of the pleasure of a happy event, but misguided or uneducated expectations can affect the quality of the new-baby experience and how prepared a woman is for it. Expectations can also create tremendous pressure and make disappointment and even depression more likely. There is opposition in all things; that opposition doesn't take a holiday when it comes to childbearing.

Hazel's experience presents a theme common to virtually all the stories shared with me:

"It just didn't feel natural, and I had such high expectations for everything to be just so natural," she told me.

Well-meaning friends and family members can inadvertently add to the burden. Hazel had a close relative impressing upon her that she had to go through labor and delivery without anesthetic—can't expose the baby to drugs—and that she had to breastfeed. Some people encourage certain methods because they're traditional, or because they believe them to be "best practices," but others convey them as matters of moral right and wrong—a woman is sinning if she chooses to do otherwise, even if other choices are forced upon her by circumstances.

Among the weightiest of expectations are the notions that motherhood comes naturally to every woman; that being responsible for another little human being should evoke only joy, not mystery and terror; that breastfeeding always happens smoothly; that patience is inexhaustible, no matter how fussy the baby and sleep-deprived the mother; and that moms automatically feel unconditional love no matter how arduous the early going is. Motherhood, we remind each other, is next to divinity. That couches within it the expectation that moms can be like God.

Some women have a baby on Tuesday and appear in church on Sunday. Even that level of divinity is woefully out of reach for most of us who have just given birth. If not physically unattainable, it is emotionally and spiritually so. But expectations—those that women impose on themselves, coupled with those supplied by family, religious belief, or the larger culture—can lead new mothers to feel that what is natural and possible *for them* is actually inadequate or even defective. Disappointment, frustration, confusion, and exhaustion are a toxic cocktail that can contribute to postpartum emotional illness.

Perhaps we forget what the scriptures actually say about expecting a baby: "Unto the woman he said, I will greatly multiply thy sorrow and thy conception; in sorrow thou shalt bring forth children" (Genesis 3:16).

And yet, this is not really the message we want to dwell on. There's a tension between the need to educate and prepare on one hand and the desire to not undermine joyful expectation on the other.

HAZEL: "At first I felt very resentful of other women, that nobody told me what life was really going to be like. At baby showers, you don't talk about how real things are. You just talk about what names you're going to choose and what color you're going to decorate the room. You talk about all these exciting things. I'm not saying you have to have a depressing baby shower, but sometimes some color of reality. But then, even for me, I try to open up to people and I try to say, if you need something. . . . How do you bring that into someone's life when they're so excited about this change in their life?"

JANE: "How do you say, 'By the way, it could be terrible'?"

HAZEL: "Yes!"

Of course we don't really want to say that. Though opposition is always possible and often present, for many, even most women, child-bearing is a joyful experience. Having a new baby is fatiguing but rewarding. But, historically, women love to share their labor and delivery stories; some careful sharing of postpartum depression experiences is not out of line in the proper context. The feeling of isolation is one of the painful manifestations of all depression, including that experienced by new mothers. Knowing that others have carried this burden and are willing to help share it in an hour of need is a blessing.

NOT BONDING WITH BABY: "IT SHOULD BE EASY FOR EVERYBODY"

Emily's second baby arrived after a quick and easy delivery. It was so easy that she momentarily thought it was going to be a breeze;

maybe they'd have lots more babies, she thought. But four days later, colic developed and the baby began crying incessantly. After a few weeks, Emily was beyond frazzled; worse still, she wasn't bonding with the baby, and she didn't feel like she could tell anyone—even her husband—about that lack of connection. "My fuse just got shorter and shorter; so much so that the second the baby opened his mouth I was handing him to someone else. I couldn't even hold him," she said.

At her six-week postpartum appointment, her OBGYN suspected she was depressed and offered to prescribe medication for it, but Emily insisted the problem was simply sleep deprivation. "I told him, 'No, I think we got this. I think we can figure this out. If he just stops crying, then I can put myself back together.'"

But the baby didn't stop crying, and he slept only in one-and-a-half-hour increments. After six months, Emily felt empty. She'd also reached the point of struggle, shared by many women, in which she was no longer seeing her OBGYN regularly and didn't know where to turn with her feelings. Lyndsey Proctor, a licensed clinical social worker in the Perinatal Outpatient Program at St. Mark's Hospital in Salt Lake City, Utah, cites the lack of continuum of care as a primary reason that women who should have been diagnosed with PPD in the early postpartum months tend to endure the pain much longer than necessary before receiving help. Do you call the OBGYN even though you're not expecting anymore? Do you show up at the emergency room? Do you tell the pediatrician at a well-baby visit? Do you get a sitter and go to your general practitioner, whom you may not have seen in years? There's precious little free time available for moms experiencing extreme stress; where should they turn when the baby is four or six months old and things aren't going well?

Emily, in fact, never went back to a doctor, and though her story did resolve happily—within another six months, she felt normal again—she still regrets that she didn't take the doctor up on his prescription offer at that six-week visit. The year-long struggle might have been months shorter had she tried medication or therapy. Part of what held her back, she believes, was her ignorance about PPD. Perhaps an even larger piece of it was her shame. "It's expected that women of the Church have babies," she says. "We are the mothers, we do this thing. If one person does it, then everybody should be able to do it. If one person makes it look that easy, then it should be easy for everybody."

Some advice from her Relief Society president during this ordeal helped alleviate these preconceived notions. "She knocked on my door, and my house was a disaster. 'Oh, Laura,' I said, 'you don't need to come in.' She goes, 'No, you need to let people in. Letting people into your house when it looks its worst is the best gift you can give. It lets them know that they're normal too.'"

Emily now knows a lot more about what's normal and what's not after pregnancy . . . and she knows about letting other people in when you're suffering. This is why Emily was willing to share parts of her experience that she'd never revealed before. It was cathartic. Today, she's a mother of three. The PPD she experienced after baby number two didn't recur with her third, but she remembers it vividly and hopes to help others who struggle with it. She worries that we might be "suffering in silence ourselves while sitting right next to someone else who is also suffering," and she wants that to end.

DISCONNECTED

When Dawn's fifth child was six months old, she began to notice what can best be described as a lack of feelings. It really perplexed her, and so she called a therapist she knew who did consultations over the phone.

"I wasn't sad and I wasn't weepy, but I didn't exist anymore. I felt like a shell," she says. "The person that I knew was past tense to me.

Prior to this, I had run a company. I had been a writer and on the board of directors. I had a lot of things going. But now I just felt completely blah. . . . I didn't even care anymore. I was like, 'Oh, that used to be me two months ago and I guess now I'm just lazy.' I just thought I was completely ambitionless. I knew something was wrong with me because I didn't feel like me, but I never would have connected it to postpartum [depression], especially since my baby was like six months old."

Numbness such as Dawn felt is one of the more surprising symptoms of PPD, says Katherine Stone, founder of PostpartumProgress .com and a leading authority on PPD. "If you think women with postpartum depression are full of strong emotions, sad, and crying all the time, and instead you feel nothing whatsoever, you may be surprised," Stone says. "Some of you tell me that you feel only emptiness. You are just going through the motions, doing the things you know you are supposed to do but not really feeling it inside. If you are disconnected from things you used to care about and it feels as if you are hovering over your life looking down on it but are no longer part of it, it's worth talking to your doctor."

When Dawn spoke with the therapist, she told her, "I don't feel like myself. I have no drive to do any of the things that used to mean anything to me." After the therapist listened to Dawn talk and suggested she might have postpartum depression, Dawn says, "I was just floored and relieved at the same time, like, 'Okay, maybe I'm not permanently broken. Maybe I haven't grown out of the person that I used to be.'"

Speaking with a therapist, taking supplements, and relying on a husband who was determined to help Dawn feel like herself again turned the tide. Within a few months, she started to feel better. Today, she wishes that there were more education about PPD. "I think it needs to be a part of birth training where you learn about the symptoms, because some of the symptoms aren't what you suspect," she says. There is, in fact, a questionnaire doctors can—and should—use to help determine if PPD might be a concern. The questionnaire is called the Edinburgh Postnatal Depression Scale, and it's widely available for both individual and clinical use.

A study published in the October 2017 issue of *Pediatrics* found that women who were screened for PPD at their child's first well-baby visit with the pediatrician were less likely to be depressed at nine months postpartum than women who were not screened. Those who are screened are more likely to get help; the sooner the need is recognized and treated, the sooner the symptoms lift.

Dawn says, "If someone had had their eye on me a little bit before, it might have been helpful." The therapist she worked with was a Latter-day Saint, which created a safe place to share her feelings about religion, too. Dawn encourages women: "If you are feeling not like yourself, go to therapy. . . . There are therapists that are completely moored in the gospel that would totally be willing to talk to you and they're trained to have eyes on it."

SLEEPLESS NIGHTS: A TIME OF LONELY INTROSPECTION

Karen was first diagnosed with postpartum depression after her third child was born. She was prescribed medication that didn't really seem to work, so when her sixth baby came along and she felt depression creeping in again, she didn't seek help, suffering through it instead. Sometimes she'd strap the kids in the car and drive because she couldn't handle more than the bare minimum at home and she had to get out. Other times, she'd get angry—a common feeling during PPD—and take it out on her husband and older kids by complaining and nagging. Sleep soon became an enemy. In its place came thoughts that she now describes as delusions. "They were not actual voices in my head," she says, "but paranoid thoughts. I was listening to those thoughts.

"I was so paranoid that one night I had all of my children and myself sleeping on our living-room floor because I said we can't go out of this room; I thought there were bad spirits around that were trying to harm us.

"It really was very dramatic. It was almost like television shows that you see."

Her husband was out of town, but "out of some miracle" her brother was in town and came over to visit. He knew something was wrong right away and took her to the hospital the next morning. She stayed for a week. She also agreed to medication and help with her sleeping issues. Unfortunately, an easy route to sleep during those awful weeks was elusive, even with help. For many women, like Karen, insomnia is one of the most frustrating symptoms of PPD. Most moms are already sleep-deprived, exhausted all day, and don't expect to have problems falling asleep when they get a chance. But with PPD, the ability to wind down and let the mind rest is often lost. Stone says, "For a woman with postpartum depression, the extra hours of lonely introspection that often accompany wakefulness in the wee hours are the last thing a mom needs."

This was very true for Karen. Her time of "lonely introspection" was filled with thoughts about all the ways she felt she had failed in life; she found herself second-guessing all the choices she'd ever made. She grew angry and frustrated, and finally, after months and months of this, she reached her breaking point one day and got in the car and just started driving. She drove thirty-six hours straight— on no sleep—thinking she would head to her parents' home on the East Coast. Somehow, she didn't fall asleep at the wheel or cause an accident, but her car did break down in western Pennsylvania. Her parents sent assistance, and she miraculously returned safely to her own home, again confronted with the need to seek professional help. The diagnosis of bipolar disorder that came next was devastating, but, thankfully, with time and practice she has learned to take care of herself in the face of chronic illness.

"I didn't want anything like this to happen ever again," she says. "I prayed really hard, and I had been praying all along, of course, but I knew that something had to change. At this point I had been taking medication, but I had to add in changing my lifestyle and my perspective and how I was living my life physically as well."

This included not cheating on sleep, not cheating on exercising, not cheating on eating, and listening to her psychiatrist. She also learned to look at things differently—as learning experiences—and rely on her testimony. "I knew Heavenly Father was aware of me and that He knew what I was going through and that He still loved me, so I could look at those things as learning experiences that we're supposed to have on Earth. I had that overall perspective, so I could look at things and say, 'Yes, this is happening to me, what can I do with this? How can I use this as something to grow from? How can I help other people?'"

She says, "I'm sure everyone has their conversation with God as well . . . why did this happen? For me the answer was that I needed to experience this so I can have greater compassion and so that I can help other people. If I look at it that way, then I don't get so bogged down, and it seems like it's a trial with a purpose rather than just a burden that I have to carry around. I can do something with it."

GUILT AND SHAME

Nina finally found the courage to ask for help when her son was eight months old and a full-blown—and terrifying—panic attack sent her to the doctor, where she also described how she'd been feeling since giving birth. "The postpartum depression was just unexplainable sadness," she says. "It was present all the time, from the moment I woke up until I went to sleep. There wasn't ever a reason for it; I just was always kind of sad and detached from my husband and from the baby. I just couldn't enjoy things like I did before he was born."

Coupled with the depression was severe anxiety, which occurs in about half the women who are diagnosed with PPD, Proctor says.

"The panic attacks were very physical for me. I would get shortness of breath and chest tightening. I'd feel like my left arm would go numb. I'd start shaking. I'd get light-headed. I'd be completely incapacitated," Nina described. It was so overwhelming that she was barely able to connect with her son or ever simply enjoy his presence. "I felt that I missed a lot of my son's first year because mentally I wasn't always as present as I could have been."

Nina was miserable. This was her first child, and the blissful days of quietly rocking a newborn that she had dreamed about before giving birth never happened. "It was really awful," she says, "because you have a bunch of ideals and expectations for what that experience of first motherhood is going to be like. And there's a lot of imagery as to what that should look like as a Mormon woman, as well. When you have postpartum depression and you're unable to feel the way that you know that you should feel and the way that you think other moms feel, there's a lot of guilt involved, a lot of shame. It's also just so disappointing and discouraging . . . because it's not what you expect or what you imagined for yourself."

When Nina weaned her baby, and her hormones leveled back out, her depression lifted. She also learned, through therapy, how to control her anxiety. Getting help was the best thing she ever did. She hopes sharing her story will encourage other women to get help.

JANE: "Where is the hope in your story, Nina? What will help other women who are struggling?"

NINA: "I think remembering is important. Remembering that you're never alone, not even for a second, that's when the hope can really reside in you. The Savior is there and He makes every experience that we go through something that is actually quite beautiful, even though it can be really difficult in the moment. We just need to remember this."

The struggle of postpartum depression transforms Isaiah's prophecy of an expected child into a much-needed beacon of hope: "For unto us a child is born, unto us a son is given . . . and his name shall be called Wonderful, Counsellor, The mighty God, The everlasting Father, The Prince of Peace" (Isaiah 9:6).

"YOU'RE NOT GETTING OUT OF BED"

Libby says "we can't do enough sharing" about postpartum depression. It is precisely because she shared her pain that Libby survived her time with PPD.

Her third child was born ten weeks early, after a diagnosis of pre-eclampsia. The post-birth shift in Libby's hormones, coupled with the stress of having a premature infant and a severe lack of sleep, triggered depression. Soon, she was having suicidal ideation and imagining all the ways she could end her life or cease to exist.

"Everything was so dark," she says. "Every move I made was slow. Every word I said was slow. It was this all-consuming darkness that just felt like there was no hope for anything ever. It was horrible. I can't describe it because it was so horrible. I can't even in my imagination make myself feel that way again."

One day, these feelings came to an apex and she decided to cut her wrists. Then reason reasserted itself, and she made herself leave her room and tell her husband she was thinking of killing herself. He went right into action.

"He called one of my friends immediately and she came over and we took a walk. She sat with me while I cried. Various people over the next few days just sat with me to make sure that I was safe. Then my husband and some of my really good friends sat down together and said, 'Okay, what's the plan?' They determined that I probably needed to be hospitalized. I'm lucky to have some friends who have gone through this and some friends who are medical professionals. They had a plan to get me to the hospital."

Libby was admitted to the general psychiatric ward at a nearby hospital. At first she was ashamed and didn't want anyone outside of her close group of friends to know, but people found out anyway. What happened was beautiful. "People came to visit me and . . . just sit and talk to me.

"People came out of the woodwork to tell me that they had had postpartum depression, that they had been hospitalized, that they were on medication. I had one woman at church who came to me and said, 'I never believed that depression was real until I had this baby.'

"We had been pregnant and were due at the same time. She ended up having her baby on time, two months after I had mine. She went through a bad stretch of postpartum. She said, 'I never believed that depression was real. I just thought you could pull yourself up by your bootstraps and you'd be fine and it was all your attitude.' She said, 'I'm on medication and it's the best thing that ever happened to me. I want to shout out from the rooftops and tell people that this is real and that there's help.'"

JANE: "How did your feelings about your experience change because of how other people responded to you? Did it help you?"

LIBBY: "Oh, it helped immensely. This is something that I think people are aware of in the periphery, but I don't think you really understand it until you've gone through it. Like I said, people came out of the woodwork and talked to me about their experiences. I realized that this is so much more prevalent than we really understand. Women need to know about this. We need to talk to each other and we need to give people the support they need when they're going through this."

JANE: "Why do you think we don't?"

LIBBY: "I think in some ways we have a cultural narrative that says women want babies and having a baby and being a mother is going to be the best part of your life. We feel ashamed of it if we find that it's not the best part of our life but it's really just a lot of poop and crying. I think that we have a tendency to focus on when things work out and the way things are supposed to be . . . rather than acknowledge that people are afraid and scared and broken. We want to believe that we are stronger than that. I think most of us in the back of our minds keep saying to ourselves, 'I can handle that. I just wake up in the morning and I'm determined and I just pull through it and I do it. I'll be okay.'

"That's even part of our American dream—our identity as Americans is that we can handle anything. A lot of hard work will just do the job. Depression is not like that. Depression doesn't care how much hard work you've done. Depression doesn't even let you do the hard work. It doesn't even let you get out of bed in the morning. You're lying in bed and saying if I could do these things I'd be okay. Depression says you're not getting out of bed."

Libby hopes anyone who is in the throes of PPD can "make that one little plea for help, that one little gasp for air and ask somebody for help." It can make all the difference.

HELPS

For those who are experiencing the trial that is postpartum depression, there is, indeed, hope. And there is help. The following are tips from the moms, doctors, and therapists I interviewed that can help ease the numbness and anxiety.

- Don't be afraid to try medication if recommended by your doctor. Lyndsey Proctor, LCSW, says that often the depression and its effects on the mother are more damaging than any risk that a medication could pose to a nursing baby.
- Don't be afraid to mother in your own way. One mom I interviewed said she just had to learn to "do me and let other moms do them." There are many ways to mother.
- Pace yourself. If you can afford it, consider hiring someone to lighten the load by helping with the baby or with housework. *Never* turn down an offer of help from a neighbor or friend.
- Go for a walk.
- Visit regularly with your doctor or therapist.
- Distract yourself by learning something new. There are all sorts of tutorials online for learning new things.
- Remember that PPD is temporary.
- Be good to yourself. Always err on the side of pampering yourself too much.
- Write in your journal. Recording your thoughts—and sleep-deprived complaints—can be therapeutic.
- Talk to a friend.
- Go out with friends.
- Ask for a priesthood blessing.

Recently, Utah Valley Hospital in Provo, Utah, announced that all new moms will be screened for "depression, anxiety, and other mental health illnesses before leaving the hospital." Employing the Edinburgh Postnatal Depression Scale, hospital personnel hope to identify risk, provide education, and initiate early treatment and therapy when needed.

This is a welcome addition to the array of care services that every maternity hospital will hopefully soon provide. In the meantime, expectant mothers should advocate for themselves in acquiring information and screening. Partners, parents, congregation members, and other concerned friends can lend help and support, lightening a new mother's load and upping the odds that she will enjoy the time she has with her new baby.

CHAPTER 8

"Agitated Horror and Relentless Despair": Suicidal Depression

*For I am persuaded, that neither death, nor life, nor angels, nor
principalities, nor powers, nor things present, nor things to come,
nor height, nor depth, nor any other creature, shall be able to
separate us from the love of God, which is in Christ Jesus our Lord.*

—Romans 8:38–39

The day that Shalese Black took her life seemed like any other day. The bright young honor student went to school, saw friends, and talked to her parents just before they left for the evening, accompanying Shalese's younger brother to receive his patriarchal blessing. She assured them she felt fine. By the time they got home, their promising eighteen-year-old daughter was gone.

On paper, Shalese's life looked perfect. Even her therapist thought so. She was driven to succeed: maintaining perfect grades in high school and participating actively in a wide range of activities and service-oriented endeavors. She was beloved by her family and friends. But beneath that veneer, Shalese felt like her mind was crumbling. Depression and anxiety, coupled with perhaps a too-strong urge to be perfect, had convinced her that she would never measure up. "She felt like she wasn't worthy or good enough for anything," her mother, Brenda, told me, "which is so strange to me, because she never did anything wrong. She was very dedicated to church and went to Young Women's every week. . . . She did have a testimony, but the depression makes it very difficult to feel the Spirit, and she felt her testimony wane as the depression got worse. It got to a point where she felt so terrible about herself that she felt she wasn't worthy to get any blessings. She even felt that God had turned on her, that He didn't love her anymore either."

That hallmark feeling of depression eventually claimed Shalese's life. Her parents later learned that friends and even one or two of her medical providers had seen glimpses of how severe Shalese's depression had become, but they hadn't told anyone, partly because of concerns about confidentiality, but perhaps also because Shalese was so good at hiding things as she continued to strive for success. After Shalese took her life, her parents decided that they would no longer hide the pain Shalese had succumbed to. They didn't want another one of God's children—any other parents' beloved child—to lose a battle with depression because they had stayed silent.

So her parents chose a most uncommon option and published Shalese's obituary without obscuring the cause of her death: "Shalese returned to her loving Heavenly Father . . . after succumbing to a long battle with depression and anxiety." Her mom says, "We feel like suicide is an epidemic right now—very much a crisis—and if we could help other people, we wanted to do so and let people know that this is a real problem."

Like Shalese's parents, I share the stories in this chapter to throw light on the societal epidemic of suicide. I have had a glimpse of this abyss. Over a period of one year, three individuals close to our family took their own lives. This issue trespasses on the most extreme emotions. It demands that those who are willing to tell their stories share the most vulnerable parts of themselves. I am humbled by their courage; unless otherwise indicated, no names have been changed.

"A BAD CHOICE BUT THE ONLY ONE": LIZZIE'S STORY

Lizzie's smile could light up a room and it often did. In high school she excelled academically, and she easily earned admission to Brigham Young University. Her days were filled with friends, hard work, and the typical rigors of college life. On paper, her life appeared perfect, and her beautiful smile forestalled questions anyone might have asked about her well-being. Her parents were aware that a bit of social anxiety had cropped up during her freshman year at BYU, but overall things were going well. Then, on a quiet fall day in 2008, Lizzie called home from Italy, where she was spending the semester abroad. "Something is wrong," she said over the phone. "I don't know what it is, Dad, but something's off—something's really wrong."

When Lizzie returned home from Europe, a number of doctors tried unsuccessfully to help her figure out what was off. Had her life proceeded normally from that point, her dad, Jim, would likely not remember that phone call. Instead, he recalls it as the beginning of a long, torturous journey that ended for Lizzie with her suicide six years later.

A little more than a year after that phone call, a second call—this one from the middle of nowhere in Central Utah—had Lizzie's dad on a plane the next day. It also finally led to some answers identifying exactly what was wrong. Lizzie made the call after days and days of sleeplessness, her mind on fire. Trying to escape, she had climbed into her car in the middle of the winter night and driven south from Provo 100 miles until she ran out of gas. She had no coat, no cell phone, no wallet. Fortunately, a highway patrol officer pulled over to help and got her on the phone with her parents.

A few days later, she was diagnosed with bipolar disorder. Its other name, manic depression, describes the two extreme and opposite phases characteristic of the disease. During manic phases— like the one that had brought her to Central Utah—Lizzie could go without sleep for days and accomplish more than usual. These phases were exhilarating but hard to hide from roommates and friends, and they terrified her with their intensity, their ability to change her personality, and their tendency to come to a grinding halt without warning. The depressive phases were even more agonizing and exhausting, resulting in declining grades, additional stress, and overwhelming feelings of worthlessness and pain. Lizzie was devastated to receive her diagnosis. She believed her future had changed dramatically.

"Suicidal depression involves a kind of pain and hopelessness that is impossible to describe—and I have tried," writes Doctor Kay Redfield Jamison, a celebrated author and professor of psychiatry at Johns Hopkins. "I teach in psychiatry and have written about my bipolar illness, but words struggle to do justice to it. How can you say what it feels like to go from being someone who loves life to wishing only to die?

"Suicidal depression is a state of cold, agitated horror and relentless despair. The things that you most love in life leach away. Everything is an effort, all day and throughout the night. There is no hope, no point, no nothing.

"The burden you know yourself to be to others is intolerable. So, too, is the agitation from the mania that may simmer within a depression. There is no way out and an endless road ahead. When someone is in this state, suicide can seem a bad choice but the only one."

At first Lizzie hoped she would somehow return to normal, that the promise of her future was still attainable and not, as Jamison described, an "endless road" with "no way out." But as the next few years passed, Lizzie became increasingly aware that her life had what she called a new baseline. Mental illness was something she would have to live with, and the unpredictability of it tormented her. Hiding it from others was all-consuming and exhausting.

"If you get cancer, you generally beat it or you die," Jim says. "With mental illness, it doesn't kill you unless you commit suicide. This is one of the challenges Lizzie had to face. She could not escape the fact that she would never get better. This used to really throw her for a loop because her practitioners, although they were sympathetic, told her, 'Unless there is some new miracle cure, we cannot cure you, Lizzie, but we can manage your symptoms.' She worried it would get much worse."

It did. Voices haunted her. She lost jobs. Over the course of a year, she was hospitalized three times—a total of fifty-five days. She turned to experimentation with prescription drugs and a little marijuana to ease the symptoms. She made several unsuccessful suicide attempts. Through it all, her parents, siblings, and boyfriend showed nothing but love for Lizzie. But the thought of living her whole lifetime with this disease—hiding it to maintain friendships and a steady job, trying new medications and enduring the debilitating side effects, believing she'd been abandoned by God—eventually overwhelmed her.

The week that Lizzie took her life began with a third never-to-be-forgotten phone call to her parents. "Nobody knew to be on guard for her mental state," her dad remembers. "In fact, just that weekend she told us everything had been going great at her job." Her treatments seemed to be working. But Lizzie was hiding the fact that she had recently lost her job and was struggling more than ever.

When Lizzie couldn't be found, her parents called the police, hoping she would be quickly and easily located. Instead, they received a return call a few hours later, the police telling them they would be coming to speak to them in person. The call told them everything. Lizzie left a note revealing that she "could just not accept the fact of where her life was going after having had such a wonderful start. She had been such a bright, bright star. She saw her life diminishing right before her eyes," Jim says.

In the last months of Lizzie's earthly life, she bookmarked a telling quote on her Pinterest board that was attributed to C. S. Lewis: "The fact that our heart yearns for something Earth can't supply is proof that Heaven must be our Home."

Each year, more than 44,000 Americans like Lizzie and Shalese yearn for something they can't find on this earth and consequently end their own lives. It is an epidemic that we can't ignore; no social or religious class is exempt. Families not only grieve the loss of loved ones but also fear they failed to do enough to save them, just one source of shame attached to the stigma of suicide.

Lizzie's parents know this all too well. Today, they've channeled some of their grief and newfound knowledge about bipolar disorder and suicide into advocacy for mental-health awareness—and especially for eliminating the stigma associated with them. At Lizzie's funeral, her family and their Latter-day Saint bishop, a world-renowned heart surgeon, openly acknowledged and explained her struggle with a "disease of the mind."

Just before what would have been her twenty-seventh birthday, the first they celebrated without her, Lizzie's family and her boyfriend designed a bright green T-shirt with #smileforlizzie printed on it. They mailed nearly six hundred of the shirts to her friends and family members all over the world along with a request that they post photos of themselves wearing the shirts on social media.

"On the day of her birthday, when those posts started coming in, it was really therapeutic," Ann says. "It was so wonderful to see so many people who shared our love for Lizzie and her memory. Some people would say, 'Why are you doing this?' It's all for parents and families to heal and to create awareness. It's what families do."

SUICIDE STATISTICS

- There was a 28 percent increase in the suicide rate in the United States from 1999 to 2016.

- Suicide is the tenth-leading cause of death in the United States.

- For every completed suicide, another twenty-five people attempt it.

- In Utah, where approximately one-third of the country's Latter-day Saints reside, suicide is the leading cause of death for young people ages 15 to 24. (It is the second-leading cause of death for ages 25 to 44 in Utah and the seventh-leading cause overall.)

- LGBTQ+ youth who are rejected by their parents are at special risk for suicide, being 8.4 times more likely than non-rejected LGBTQ+ youth to attempt suicide. (Additionally, they report high levels of depression at six times the rate of nonrejected youth.)

- White males die by suicide 3.5 times more than women.

- Women attempt suicide three times as often as men.

- A 70 percent increase in suicide rate among girls was reported from 2010 to 2016.

- Firearms account for 49.8 percent of suicide deaths.

- Forty percent of those who die by suicide had made a previous attempt.

- Suicide costs the United States $51 billion annually.

"WHAT FAMILIES DO": WHAT CHURCH DOCTRINE SAYS ABOUT SUICIDE

As members of a Church that has the eternal family at the center of its doctrine, Latter-day Saints often feel left adrift, uncertain what suicide means for a loved one's salvation and their own family's eternal status. The stinging stigma attached to mental illness and suicide aggravates the already intense pain of grief. Questions plague the mind. Church leaders have historically provided words that bring a measure of peace, comfort, and hope to families tortured by the suicide of a loved one. Until recently, however, little had been said specifically and authoritatively about the eternal and doctrinal ramifications of suicide.

Then, in July 2018, the Church released a series of videos addressing this very topic and vocalizing a pressing need to do all we can to prevent suicide, to minister to those who have suicidal thoughts or who have attempted suicide, and to support those who are left behind when a loved one does take his or her life.

"Every one of us," Elder Dale G. Renlund of the Quorum of the Twelve Apostles says, "has family members, dear friends, or acquaintances who have experienced suicidal thoughts, attempted suicide, or have taken their lives—and every time is tragic.

"We know, from all the statistics out there, that someone in the ward is hurting, someone is having suicidal thoughts in *your* ward. And as we come together as families, as churches, in a community, we can do better than we're doing now. This is the way that we decrease any kind of embarrassment, reduce any kind of stigma, and gain further understanding about the process.

"There's an old sectarian notion that suicide is a sin and that someone who commits suicide is banished to hell forever. *That is totally false!* I believe the vast majority of cases will find that these individuals have lived heroic lives and that suicide will not be a defining characteristic of their eternities.

"I think Heavenly Father is pleased when we reach out and help His children. I think He's profoundly pleased. . . . We shouldn't underestimate the importance of the Church as a community coming together and helping each other through this life. Heavenly Father knew it would be a challenge and He knew we would need each other's help. So, what we need to do as a Church is to reach out in love and caring for those who have suicidal thoughts, who have attempted suicide, who feel marginalized in any way. We need to reach out with love and understanding."

"A PLACE IN THE CELESTIAL KINGDOM": GEORGE H. BRIMHALL'S STORY

One telling story about the aftermath of suicide is that of George H. Brimhall, one of the greatest educators in the history of the Church. He served as president of Brigham Young University for seventeen years and once said, "Education is more than preparing for life. It is life." He reared thirteen children to maturity and served in dozens of Church callings, working relentlessly to educate young people. At the time of his death, he had written more lessons for the Young Men's Mutual Improvement Association than any other person. Ten years before Brimhall's death, President Heber J. Grant wrote to him, declaring: "I know of no single worker . . . who has put more genuine thought and study and has done more work for the advancement of our young men than your own dear self. I am wondering, my dear brother, if you . . . have been guilty of over-doing."

But even as he selflessly dedicated himself to others, Brimhall suffered greatly. He lost two children under the age of three. A dear brother died by a lightning strike while tending his crops. Two years after the birth of their sixth child, his first wife was admitted to the state mental hospital in Provo, where she lived the remainder of her life—forty-two years. He dealt with many health issues of his own. An article in the *Provo Herald* announcing his death reported that "members of his family observed that [Brimhall] had grown discouraged and that his restless spirit chafed under the long siege which had sapped his strength." Of course, we can never know exactly what was going through his mind or his body at the time of his death, but we do know that whatever it was, it was enough to cause him to seek out a rifle in his home and end his life with a single shot to the head.

His death devastated his colleagues in the Church education community, his family, and the Church in general. John A. Widtsoe, a fellow educator, president of the Church's European Mission, and later a member of the Quorum of Twelve Apostles, heard of Brimhall's death while traveling in Europe and expressed concerns about the speculative talk surrounding it. He wrote to his friend (and Brimhall's successor at Brigham Young University), Franklin S. Harris, "Is there anything I should know to assist in turning the gossip that seems to be spreading among the missionaries of this mission?" He was troubled that members of the Church would do anything but grieve and respect this great man.

Harris wrote back, "Certainly this was a very tragic affair but I think no one who knows all the circumstances blames President Brimhall for the occurrence any more than if he had fallen from a horse or if he had been overcome by any other disaster for which he was in no way responsible." At the funeral, Elder George Albert Smith, who himself suffered from depression, said: "It must be a source of great satisfaction to those who call him 'husband' and 'father' to know that he has gone home; that his work is complete; that he has not gone to be idle, but to continue to do good. . . . He has gone home. Not to some obscure, undesirable place. He has been working for a place in the Celestial Kingdom. He has been seeking to have his name recorded in the Lamb's Book of Life. And I believe that if any man has accomplished that desirable thing, George H. Brimhall has accomplished it."

Long respected in the Church for his gospel knowledge and erudition, Elder James E. Talmage, like George Brimhall an educator as well as a churchman, wrote in his journal that "I am sure the man was wholly irresponsible and that every circumstance will be taken into account in the final judgment as to his splendid life and sudden death."

TALKING ABOUT SUICIDE
AND MENTAL ILLNESS

If Brimhall's story and Elder Renlund's pleas to help convey one principle, it is that it is not our place to judge. It is our place to love. It is our place to grieve. And it is our place to mourn with those who suffer from the dark feelings of suicidal ideation and those who are left behind when those feelings result in action. This is one of the most difficult losses a family can experience. It should harrow up our deepest feelings of compassion and stir us up from the sidelines to active, truly charitable, and supportive sharing of its crushing burden. There is no place for condemnation, gossip, or shunning. There is room for prevention, for communication, and—always—for the Atonement of Jesus Christ.

Suicide should not be swept under a rug. Just as it is never good to box up and ignore our feelings, it is never good to keep silent about suicidal thoughts and mental health in general. The notion that talking to someone about their feelings may lead people to act on them has been debunked by a number of studies, as well as by those who have unsuccessfully attempted suicide themselves and are now healing. Talking about suicide can actually help prevent it. When I spoke with Dr. Thomas Damaria, a psychologist with the National

Center for School Crisis and Bereavement, he explained: "Whether it's a stressor that they're dealing with causing them a lot of shame, or whether there's a hopeless situation that they feel they can't get out of, . . . airing it out and talking to somebody can help [them] start to problem solve and come up with better solutions. We find that often-times the journey of suicide is one of a narrowing of focus and a nar-rowing of possibilities, and it's kind of a tunnel vision where people don't see out of that little tunnel that they get caught in. Often that tunnel is promoted by depression, and depression is all about feeling helpless and hopeless and powerless. Talking to another person and having the person help you problem solve and look for alternative solutions, reasons for living, protective factors that can help keep you safe, can actually prevent suicide from occurring."

Dr. Damaria emphasized to me that "talking about suicide does not cause people to commit suicide. Not talking about it, neglecting to talk about it, sends the message that they *can't* talk about it. It's im-portant to talk about feelings of depression, or other fantasies about suicide, which can certainly fester inside, if they're not talked about more openly."

Elder Renlund, who is also a medical doctor, echoes this and pro-vides specific direction for us, as Latter-day Saints, to help others: "It's completely safe, completely safe to ask someone if they're having sui-cidal thoughts or if they are having thoughts of harming themselves. The most important thing—if one's a friend—is to make sure one gives adequate time to listen."

A great way to do this, Elder Renlund says, is to "reach out and hold them by the hand, look them in the eyes, and ask, 'Have you thought of harming yourself?' And if they pause for a long time and say, 'Maybe,' that should raise the red flag. This is now beyond that they need to read the scriptures or pray more fervently or exercise more faith. Those things will become important, but right now you need more help. . . . If you genuinely love the person, then you're willing to sit there with them, and you're willing to cry with them, and you're willing to hold them. And you do that in concert with healthcare professionals and with ecclesiastical leaders, with friend and family support. In most cases, people continue to have a burden. But the burden can be made lighter."

There can be no dispute: nothing but love and compassion—totally devoid of judgment—should be bestowed upon individuals who live with and die from mental illness. You can never know what is going on inside a depressed person's head. Abby, the grieving older sister of teenaged Spencer—who ended his life after a battle with depression—told me, "I don't think you ever really realize what people are dealing with unless you're really inside their head. For someone like Spencer, who had everything going for him, I mean really, everything you could imagine, he had going for him. The fact that someone as amazing as him would commit suicide. It could be anyone. You really have to be kind and understanding of other people. Help them to get what they need because you never really know where people are." That loving kindness should be extended with equal generosity to the families who survive them.

Abby also provides insight into the burden that often *precedes* a suicide: a heavy responsibility—at times being shouldered by very young children—associated with even knowing the risk exists. "Depression is something that runs in my family. It's something that my grandmother had struggled with. My dad and all his siblings have depression as well. It's something I struggle with as well, so it wasn't really a shock to me when I started to realize that my brother struggled with it. Actually, when he was about twelve, he told me, just in passing but in the strictest confidence, that he had thought about suicide for a really long time and it was something that he really struggled with. I finally told my mom."

Her mother, Marion, expands on Abby's concern about the careful balance of protecting a loved one's privacy while still addressing the person's need. It is an effort imbued with fear and feelings of helplessness, particularly when there has been active suicidal ideation or, as in Spencer's case, a suicide attempt. "It was only kept inside of our family. We didn't tell anyone really outside of our immediate family . . . just the six of us. A few people, but very, very few. Maybe three knew, outside of the circle of the six of us, what had gone on. We were trying everything that we possibly could. For the longest time, he wasn't even allowed to be alone. We monitored him, even when he'd go into his room, his brother—they shared a room—but he would go in there, and say, 'Oh, I just need to come in and read a book.'"

It should be noted, too, that Spencer was receiving counseling and other therapy. In many cases, families are aggressively pursuing every possible means to save a life, just as we do when confronted with other potentially terminal illnesses. Nevertheless, the feeling that they could and should have done more is a uniquely cold companion in the aftermath of a death from mental illness, seldom experienced to the same extreme degree when a loved one dies from more "natural" causes.

As Eric Dyches, whose wife, Emily, lost her battle with postpartum depression and anxiety, put it, "I want us to have ultra-mercy for the survivors, because people in our culture carry heavy, heavy burdens when a family member takes their life. I think it's completely contrary to the gospel of Christ that we would look at that individual and somehow label the survivor because their family member took their life. We don't have all the parts to the equation, and God is the ultimate judge, but I know that families carry heavy burdens because of the way they perceive people looking at them, the culture."

LEFT BEHIND: CHASE AND LUCY'S STORY

Owning the pain of depression and finding ways to heal while talking about the epidemic of suicide is something Lucy is intimately familiar with. On a quiet winter afternoon, I sat in Lucy's beautiful living room and asked this dear friend to share with me the most painful experience of her life. Lucy's adult son, Chase, took his life during what can only be described as an out-of-the-blue, acute psychotic episode. At the time, he was taking a medication for sleep for which suicidal ideations and behavior are listed as possible side effects. It is not definitive, however, that those side effects caused his death. It's unclear, even, to what extent Chase was suffering from depression.

The story I share here of Chase's death could go in many directions: What are pharmaceutical companies doing about the medications that have these severe side effects? Why take such medications in the first place? Could Chase's death have been prevented? What led to his death? Sadly, none of these questions have satisfactory answers. Any answer would be complicated and clinical, shedding little light on Chase as an individual child of God, loved by his family, friends, and Heavenly Father.

What follow instead are excerpts from my interview with Chase's mother, providing a tender glimpse at those left behind when someone commits suicide, their *own* vulnerability to depression, how they move forward, and where they find the spiritual strength to continue to believe.

When Lucy, a widow and a convert to the Church of seventeen years, knelt to pray the morning of Chase's death, she already knew something was very wrong with her son. "As I knelt, that morning of his death, I felt that something ominous was going to happen. I knelt at my bed, and I prayed, and I cried to the Lord to take care of Chase."

She left immediately to make the several-hours' drive to Chase's home in New Hampshire, talking to him on the phone as she drove.

150

"I kept saying, 'Chase, something is very wrong. Please let me talk to you. Please let us get together.'" Chase's responses were flat and non-committal. By the time Lucy arrived, he had already taken his life. It was that fast, like a rushing locomotive that couldn't be slowed, she recalls. "As a mother, that's a hard pill to swallow, when we realize that, as much as we love our children, we can't always protect them."

Lucy felt tortured at first; dark thoughts filled her mind: "I felt that somehow I could have stopped it. Somehow, I could have stopped my child's illness. Somehow I could have changed something in the way we nurtured, engaged in this child . . ."

JANE: "You've told me before about how the depression *you* experienced after Chase died colored everything else in your life."

LUCY: "I think we look at life through dark lenses. Certainly, after Chase died, I had a very hard time sleeping. . . . I consider myself an active person who likes to be involved in many things, but I was barely managing, barely functioning. It was through the help of grief counselors and, ultimately, medication. Having a medical background, I knew that functioning on two hours of sleep was ultimately going to do harm to my physical body, much less my mental state."

JANE: "Do you think Chase was depressed?"

LUCY: "I've thought about it a lot. I've had more than a year to think about it. If he was, he was pretty high-functioning. The best comment I can give you on that is I will never know for sure. Part of me goes back to scriptures when the Lord says, 'My ways are not your ways, my thoughts are not your thoughts' [see Isaiah 55:8].

"It's very hard not knowing the answers, but I've learned from grief counseling that I will never get the answer. At some point, I just have to move on. I think as a Latter-day Saint, what gives me comfort is that in a month, Chase, who had just started college when we joined the Church, will be posthumously baptized by his brother, and confirmed. He will be sealed to us as a family. . . . That's the beauty of the gospel. I know that to be true. I feel it. As much as I want him here with me, knowing that he is without pain, with his dad, whom he adored, it's a great comfort to me."

JANE: "What about the other emotions you've felt as part of this experience? I think sometimes people are afraid to feel hard things, some of the really hot emotions. The difficult ones that make us feel uncomfortable."

LUCY: "Oh, sure. I've had those. There are times when I've been angry at Chase, saying, 'If this had been bugging you, why didn't you call me? Why didn't you see someone?' On the other side of that, I've often thought, what did I miss in my mothering of him that maybe didn't allow him to come to me? Sometimes I've been angry at him for taking a permanent solution to a temporary problem. I also go to the drug companies. . . . The facts online are pretty devastating. This is pretty serious stuff. There are times when I've been questioning God, saying, 'I do my best, I'm not the perfect Latter-day Saint, but I pay my tithing, I go to church, I serve at the temple. What did you need for me to learn from this? I got on my knees that morning, and I begged you to save Chase. Were you listening to me? Did you hear me?'

"Sure, I get angry. And I have felt impotent, that I couldn't help him. I think it's all part of the grieving process. I think there are steps in the grieving process. We don't all go through them at the same time. From what I've read, and what I've been counseled, you have to get through the process. As ugly and as uncomfortable as it is, there's no way but through it. There's just no way but through it."

LETTING THE SAVIOR TAKE YOUR BURDEN: TANYA'S STORY

I spoke with another woman of great courage—a woman who understands far too well the idea that "there's no way but through it"—just a year after her second attempt to take her own life. Our conversation was deeply moving. And, despite the heavy topic, there were moments of lightness and an overriding feeling of hope.

Getting to this point, however, was not easy. Depression had made its first big reveal in Tanya's life a decade earlier, when her small-town doctor diagnosed her with major depressive disorder. She spent the next six months in the lowest state of mind she could have possibly imagined at the time, rarely getting off the couch and at one point going two weeks without a shower. Spiritually, she felt as if she were already dead inside.

"There just wasn't anything," she said. "I felt like I'd been abandoned. I'd always felt like depression was something that happened because you were doing something wrong and that the Lord wasn't with you anymore—that He left you alone because you weren't doing the right things. But I never knew what that was, and so I was always trying harder to be that person that I thought I needed to be, but I never was."

Things got progressively worse, until one day she decided everyone in her life would be better off without her. She found one of her husband's guns in the house. But she also made a phone call to her sister-in-law, who insisted that Tanya stay on the phone until help arrived. That call saved her life. Her sister-in-law took her to a big-city psychiatrist in a town 150 miles away. There, Tanya was diagnosed with bipolar disorder and learned that the medication she'd been taking for the previous six months was not effective for manic depression. No wonder she'd not felt any better.

In an ideal world, this would have been a turning point for Tanya, but life is anything but ideal. For the next ten years, she tried one medication after another, none of them ever working just right. Even so, there were some good moments and a few lessons learned.

I asked Tanya specifically how her loved ones reacted.

TANYA: "My ex-husband, he didn't want to be educated in what was going on, you know. And some family members were really old-school, where depression is where you just pray and read your scriptures and you should be fine. And so they didn't really understand what I was going through."

"It was my grandfather, who is now in his nineties, who actually called me and talked to me about it. And he understood 100 percent; he talked a little bit about my great-grandfather, who also had bipolar disorder, and who had taken his own life. And he was very understanding and called me every day and checked on me. And so he was kind of my safe place, I should say."

Her grandfather's call after her first suicide attempt and his calls in the subsequent months—along with new medications to treat manic depression specifically—helped sustain her.

Then the medications stopped working, and her husband asked for a divorce. "That was the point where I got down to that place again," Tanya says. That place was so dark that she made a plan. She knew what, when, and where she was going to do it. She came home from work and took all of her medications. At once. One hundred fifty pills.

Tanya suffered a seizure and ended up in the intensive care unit at the hospital, followed by several months at a recovery center. It was there that a turning point was reached—a turning point with Christ at its center. During the previous ten years of struggling with manic depression, Tanya had harbored the thought that this was something she should be able to solve on her own, that the depression might even be partly her fault.

At the recovery unit, Tanya met daily with a therapist who helped her confront these notions head-on. The therapist happened to be Christian and very well-versed in the Bible. Knowing her faith, he read Tanya the words from Matthew 11:28—"Come unto me, all ye that labour and are heavy laden, and I will give you rest."

And then he asked her this question: "Do you really believe that Christ felt all those feelings that you're feeling, and that He can take your infirmities upon Him, and that He will lighten your burden if you were to just go to Him?"

She thought about that for a good, long time and then said, "You know what? I don't know if I really do believe that." She realized that she'd been feeling like this depression was something she would suffer her whole life and even beyond, that there was no hope of relief—no light at the end of any tunnel. She believed her feelings were wrong and must be kept hidden from the world. Hidden, even, from her Savior.

Her therapist told her to take it one step at a time and pray first about the Atonement of Christ and about how she fit into that. "And so I did," Tanya says, "and he asked me next time he saw me to pray that I could let go of my pride. And I thought, 'Well, that's kind of a weird thing,' you know? But he said, 'You need to let go of that pride to be able to let Him into your life. And you do need help from Him.'

"And so it actually took me a couple weeks to get to where I felt that I could give those burdens to Him. . . . At that point my therapist asked me to pray to tell the Savior that this was too hard for me and I needed Him to carry those burdens for me.

"And I did, I prayed for that; and probably on about day five of praying about that, I really felt like He had taken that burden. Maybe not all the way, but enough that I could function, and I could feel like there was some hope, and feel like I knew . . . I just knew that I had a place in this world and that I did matter, and that He was there always to take those burdens from me if it was too hard. And when I got done I looked back at it and I realized that through those times, those dark times, He was carrying me. But I just couldn't see it. I didn't want to see it. And I feel like He's carried me for the last ten years. I just never really saw it until then."

WHEN SUICIDE FEELS LIKE THE HAPPIEST OPTION: KAYDEN'S STORY

No conversation about depression and suicide would be complete without sharing the challenges of Church members who identify as gay or are otherwise part of the LGBTQ+ community.

Suicide rates for children ages twelve to eighteen are frighteningly high. A 2015 study by the Centers for Disease Control (CDC) reported that 8.6 percent of high-school students had attempted suicide (17 percent had considered it). For adolescents who identify as lesbian, gay, or bisexual, however, the percentage was *more than triple* that (the study did not look at those who identify as transgender): 29.4 percent of LGB students had attempted suicide and 42.8 percent had seriously considered it. Just over 60 percent of LGB teens had reported feeling "so sad or helpless every day for 2 or more weeks in a row that they stopped doing some usual activities." Undoubtedly, there are a number of Latter-day Saint LGB youth included in these percentages.

Kayden was one of them. Though his story does not provide answers to the questions many gay and lesbian members have about their place in the Church, it is a peek into a life experience that few of us adequately understand. By age fourteen, Kayden recognized that he did not have the same feelings for girls as other boys his age did. At first, he didn't comprehend exactly what that meant for his future. In fact, he initially thought, "I'll just take care of it with the bishop, one on one . . . and fix myself and then no one else would have to know."

But Kayden fell into a deep depression as he realized that he would never be able to live the life he had always dreamed of. "You sing songs about it in Primary, you learn lesson after lesson about how to have a happy family. . . . It's a beautiful plan and it's wonderful, and I would've done anything to hold to that. [But] as soon as you accept that you're gay, it suddenly complicates things dramatically."

In his journal, Kayden made a list of pros and cons regarding the four paths he believed he could take: (1) leave the Church, gain the opportunity to have a companion and children—but feel like a sinner; (2) marry a woman and together strive for the ideal family life he wanted—but feel like a fraud; (3) remain celibate and wait for the afterlife—when, as he'd often been told, "everything would all work out"; or (4) end his life immediately to hasten the outcome of option three.

Kayden's conclusion after reviewing the pros and cons of each path is heart wrenching: the fourth option.

JANE: "You felt like suicide was the only answer?"

KAYDEN: "It wasn't the only answer, but it was the happiest one. I was suffocating just looking at my own future and what was lying in front of me. It just started to feel like I had nothing to look forward to in this life."

Kayden's mom, Tammy, describes the struggle that ensued, "the depth of self-hatred. . . . He just really thought the best thing was for him to move on to the next life. . . . He believed that God had made a mistake."

The years that followed were fraught with worry and despair for both Tammy and Kayden. They talked openly to one another about *everything,* which allowed Tammy to gain insight into Kayden's feelings while also keeping him as safe as she could. He saw a therapist who helped him work through many things. At times, Kayden felt supported by his Latter-day Saint peers at school, but at other times he felt bullied by them. His depression worsened during his senior year. Though Kayden had previously been a straight-A student, he stopped going to classes and almost didn't graduate.

Tammy tearfully recalls the terror of those days, the constant fear that her son would not survive his deep depression. "There were times I feared going downstairs to his bedroom because I didn't know what I would find. I didn't want to send his younger brother and sister down without me because I didn't want them to find him."

Tammy may not have realized it at the time, but the younger children she was protecting were also the reason Kayden did not take the fateful final action.

JANE: "Why didn't you do it?"

KAYDEN: "My little siblings, actually. I just couldn't really leave them behind. I love them so much."

Tammy still worries about getting a call informing her that Kayden has taken his own life. Perhaps she always will. Her fear for her son's well-being and feelings of helplessness have precipitated her own depression, which she continues to battle. "He wants to belong so bad. It just breaks my heart over and over and over. . . . I can't get over the loneliness that I feel for him that I know he feels—that just wanting to belong."

Today, Kayden hopes that the worst crisis has passed. He left the Church for a different faith community not long after a gay acquaintance died by suicide, but he says he isn't hostile. "I had a really positive experience with the Church. My ward was so welcoming and my bishop was so kind, and I didn't leave because people were cruel to me; I left because I did not feel comfortable with the options that lay ahead of me. . . .

"Every single story we read about [Jesus Christ], He's extending love to people who don't feel like they deserve it and He's reaching out an arm to people that society has cast out.

"I know my intent and God knows my intent . . . and that's all right."

The words *suicide* and *hope* sit together oddly on the page. Suicide is, after all, what happens when someone loses hope; it is the ultimate act of despair. But there is always hope. Tanya finds it through prayer and sessions with a therapist willing to spend long hours working not only on her mental health but on her spiritual health as well. Kayden finds it through the love of his family and confidence that the Lord loves him too, and loves him not *despite* his sexual orientation but because he is a child of God like any other. Lucy finds it through the blessings of the temple that have now sealed her family eternally, reassurance that she is forever bonded to her son Chase and will see him again. Marion, mother of Spencer, expresses her hope with heartbreaking honesty: "To feel like there's such a different way that you can look at this situation that it doesn't have to be negative. It will hurt and there is no doubt that there will be pain involved, but it doesn't have to be a negative. It can be turned into a positive where we learn from the experience and we grow from it and we're better because of it and we make the lives of other people better because of it.

"I believe I'm being taught by my grief, by my son, by my Heavenly Father, by the people around me."

Testifying of the holy Resurrection that will raise weak things into power, Elder Jeffrey R. Holland implores those struggling with mental illness to trust in God and hold onto His love: "I bear witness of that day when loved ones whom we knew to have disabilities in mortality will stand before us glorified and grand, breathtakingly perfect in body and mind. What a thrilling moment that will be! I do not know whether we will be happier for ourselves that we have witnessed such a miracle or happier for them that they are fully perfect and finally 'free at last.'"

CHAPTER 9

"I Just Want to Help": For Families and Friends

For now we see through a glass, darkly; but then face to face: now I know in part; but then shall I know even as also I am known. And now abideth faith, hope, charity, these three; but the greatest of these is charity.

—1 Corinthians 13:12–13

In the course of my career as a journalist, I've traveled the world to interview everyone from heads of state and Hollywood stars to the proverbial men and women on the street. I've conducted interviews in war zones and places devastated by natural disaster. I conducted hundreds of interviews, many of them heartbreaking, to research and write this book. But I think it's fair to say that the hardest interview I've ever done was the one I conducted in my own living room with my husband, Mark.

JANE: "So, I want to talk to you about what it was like for you to live with someone who suffered with depression."

MARK: "I'm a little fearful of this conversation."

JANE: "You shouldn't be."

MARK: "Really? What if I say something that's hard to hear?"

JANE: "I am speaking outside of myself right now as a reporter and I want you to be very honest. Do you remember the first time you thought, 'Huh, she might have a little depression'?"

MARK: "Yes. I remember this image of you on the front porch. I have no idea what the issue was, but you were hunched over, and I realized at that moment that clinically something was wrong. It was so clear in your face and in your eyes that you were in a different place."

JANE: "What was it like for you, as my husband, to go through that one really bad depressive episode?"

MARK: "For me, depression tapped into some of my deepest emotions—anger, hurt, frustration, sadness, fear. I felt frustrated because I wanted to fix it, and unhappy because I couldn't reach you. I experienced it as a frontal assault. I took it personally, like I had done something wrong, or I had let you down in some way. I just wanted it to stop. But I remember thinking so many times, why is this happening? I want my wife back."

JANE: "What was it like to be in the middle of a storm, when the storm is a depressed person who is crying and angry and sad and miserable and sleeping all the time . . . who can't really perform basic life functions?"

MARK: "To be brutally honest, my logical brain kept saying, 'Why can't she just snap out of this? She could get out of this if she wanted to.' Sometimes I thought I could talk you out of it. Remember that? Finally I realized, 'Oh, this is a really bad disease and I don't understand it.'

"It mostly felt to me like you were such a different person. You enclosed. Everything turned inward, and there was no connection. I have such love for you, and we have such an intimacy. But with the depression, all of a sudden our synching was completely gone. It felt like a separation, like you're now this person that I don't have any connection with and can't really reach or reason with. In those moments, I felt really scared."

JANE: "Scared?"

MARK: "Yes. Scared I might never get you back."

JANE: "So what would you tell someone who's going through this, who has never experienced depression and who's seeing it from the outside, looking in?"

MARK: "That this too will pass. And that you can't take it personally. You need to be understanding and loving and supportive, but you don't have to be a punching bag, either. And that you shouldn't try to fix it. In a sense, I think by going through that with you, I built my own ability to be more expressive. I don't look at your experience— our experience—as a negative for our family. We've definitely grown because of this."

If you are a spouse, a child, a parent, a sibling, or a friend of someone who is depressed, this chapter is for you. You are a victim of depression just like the person you care about and want to help. I know that you sometimes—even often—feel hopeless and hurt. I want to reassure you that your love matters and you *can* help— but I also know how hard and thankless your lot is. What I share here won't lift your burden entirely, but if it lightens it even a little through renewed hope, I will have accomplished my purpose. There is much we can do to accentuate hope when we come into contact with mentally ill people and their families.

Depression destroys relationships, from the outside in and from the inside out. As Andrew Solomon wrote in his award-winning book *The Noonday Demon,* depression drives its sufferers so deep into themselves that it "ultimately eclipses the capacity to give or receive affection." From the outside, depression looks a lot like selfishness and can feel like rejection and abandonment.

As one who has wrestled this demon, I attest that it looks and feels that way from the inside as well. A friend of mine once told me, "Depression is a ball and chain. Some people drag it. Other people swing it." I fall into the latter category; when I swung the ball, I took direct aim at the people I love the most. No one wants to make loved ones unhappy, but I know that when I was in the bondage of depression, that's exactly what I did.

This is common in relationships in which one person is mentally ill and the other fills the roll of caregiver. A depressed person is, bluntly, difficult to love. Sadly, when compassion fatigue sets in, many relationships don't survive. The interviews I conducted revealed occasions of angry arguments, of children and spouses who felt abandoned, of parents who mourned their children's lost futures. At least one woman I interviewed, who described her difficult but to that point successful journey supporting her depressed spouse, has since divorced and left the Church. But those are not the stories I want to tell. Instead, this chapter is about relationships that *have* survived, why they've survived, and what has gone right—but sometimes wrong—along the way. It's my hope that their stories will provide insight and comfort to you who watch, worry, and work endlessly from the other side of depression's dark glass.

"THE THINGS I GOT WRONG"

More than twelve years ago, I read a touching post on a popular blog about everything the writer had done wrong when he first responded to his wife's depression. Tom and his wife had been married only five years when he wrote the article, but it was filled with insight, hope, and positivity. Among the things he says he got wrong:

"Early in our marriage I was attached to the idea that happiness is a choice. Unhappiness, I thought, could be cured by adjusting attitude and seeking the Spirit. This way of thinking worked for me (and it mostly still does) and I saw no reason that it shouldn't work for my wife. So when she had problems I explained to her the way that I thought and expected her to just choose to be better. When she didn't, I saw it as a character flaw (I blamed her). I don't think I ever told her this, but she sensed it. This attitude of mine made her feel worse. Rather than being understanding and compassionate I ended up being obtuse and accusatory. Also unhelpful was pointing out to her that her feelings were irrational. She already knew that."

Ironically, but surprisingly common in relationships, Tom's second "wrong" was the counterpoint of his first. "I blamed myself. Any time my wife broke down and told me about the kinds of thoughts she was having it made me feel like a complete failure," he wrote. "She told me many times that I wasn't the source of her problems. But when she told me that she had suicidal thoughts, it was difficult not to think that it was because I was making her life miserable. I resented her sometimes for telling me these things because it made me feel like I couldn't make any mistakes without sending her over the edge, like I had to constantly walk on eggshells."

I tracked Tom down while researching this book to ask for his impressions now, how his wife is doing, and how things have changed in the dozen years since he'd written the article. Today, Tom and his wife have four children and have been married more than seventeen years. Tom says he wouldn't change anything about the blog post; the advice he gave—and the things he did wrong—remain the same. His wife still deals with depression and anxiety, but they've learned techniques together to help manage it and endure the rough spots.

He explains how his blaming his wife's attitude early on aggravated her depression: "When I was judging her . . . it made her feel that she was not living up to some gospel standard. Part of the problem was she already had this . . . fear that the bad thoughts that she was having were sins in and of themselves and therefore made her unworthy of God's love, of the celestial kingdom, of the Spirit. My judgment added on top of that just validated what she was already feeling, her negative feelings and her negative fears about herself. It was really compounding the problem rather than solving it."

He's learned to resist the trap of self-blame when his wife isn't well. "It is important for loved ones on the outside looking in to not take a loved one's struggles with depression as a sign of your own failure. When your spouse is depressed, it's hard not to think that you are a cause of the unhappiness, that you are failing in some way to make them happy. I have sometimes reflexively felt defensive when my wife has shared her struggles with me, as if she was accusing me of not being loving enough or supportive enough. When that happens, I have to remind myself that her illness is not my fault, just as it is not her fault."

Today, Tom blames depression—not people—when things go awry. This behavior took a while to learn, but it helps tremendously, as does simply loving the depressed person. As you'll see from Tom's story (and the others in this chapter), the decisive variable in relationship survival is love. Andrew Solomon writes, "Depression is a disease of loneliness"; love is an essential remedy in its treatment. Not, he adds, because it "ameliorates the symptoms of depression (it does not), but because it gives people evidence that life may be worth living if they can only get better. It gives them a place to admit to their illness, and admitting it is the first step toward resolving it."

Tom and I discussed many things, but this point is most important: "Marriage to a person with mental illness is not doomed to be miserable." Tom and his wife make their marriage work despite her depression. "We have had struggles, especially early on when I was not as understanding and supportive as I should have been. But I have what I consider to be a happy marriage, and I'm glad for the choice I made. I wouldn't say I'm glad my wife sometimes struggles with anxiety and depression, but I am grateful for the experiences we've shared and for the chance I've had to become more understanding and compassionate. When both spouses are committed to love and care for one another, it is possible to build something great together."

The responses to Tom's blog post more than ten years ago were also instructive. Some readers commented on the agony and isolation that can encompass a caregiving spouse. Others suggested approaches that help them ride out the rough times with spouses who have depression. This anonymous comment echoes many of the sentiments expressed by those I interviewed: "When things first started really going south for us, I got what I believe is the best advice for any caregiver—spouse, friend, priesthood leader, anyone. That was to not let my wife's struggles destroy my life. Do everything I can to make my personal life as normal as I can. Keep my same interests, hobbies, etc. The better shape I am in, the better I can help my wife.

"The advantage to that is, when it works, it helps my wife keep her morale up. She tells me often that she thinks she is ruining my life. If I can point out to her all the good things that I have held on to, I can talk her out of that notion. On the other hand, when I let it get to me, she takes full blame for my bad days."

Depression can—and often does—seem like a mask overlying your loved one's true and former self. Feeling that "this is not the person I know" is typical, but depression shouldn't be allowed to also subvert a *caregiver's* authentic self.

LETTING SOMEONE ELSE TAKE THE REINS

Rob has depression; he's also afflicted with anxiety and obsessive-compulsive disorder (OCD). This toxic combination has, at times, cost him employment and makes it difficult to attend church or visit places that are loud and crowded. Fortunately, both his wife and his bishop have been supportive and innovative in finding ways to help.

The bishop, for example, called Rob as the ward financial clerk, a calling he can fulfill alone in a quiet office, with the door closed. The bishop also offered valuable advice when Rob's depression led to scrupulosity and he worried that every little thing he did was wrong or unrighteous.

"My wife stepped in and we sat down with the bishop," Rob says, "and I explained how stupid things would make me feel like I was going to hell: if I ate too much dinner, if I forgot to get the mail. If I did things like that, I would feel just horrible, like I had ruined everything, and not just ruined everything for the day, but it was that I had ruined everything for our happy life. The bishop's advice was, he said, 'Rob, I don't want you to think about where you're going to end up in heaven.' He said, 'I think what you need to do is put your faith in your wife, and let her be the spiritual leader of the family. When she feels a prompting, you listen to it, and because you have faith in your wife, then you will know that it is coming from God.'"

Rob is doing much better now, but this advice, and his wife's ability to take the reins and shoulder the mantle the bishop suggested, carried Rob through some rough years. "I put everything in her hands," Rob told me, "and if she thought that I was doing something wrong, then she would let me know. If we had to make a big life decision, I would defer to her and the testimony that she had. That was hard, but my wife is totally the one who has gotten me through this mental illness, and I am just very grateful that I can look to her whenever I need. Right now, I'm at the point where I'm back, and I can receive answers from prayers, but there was a long time where it was very frightening and I couldn't do it."

When Rob's wife took on the spiritual mantle in their relationship, her actions softened the isolation he felt as he was, so to speak, wandering in a spiritual wilderness. It also demonstrated that everything a righteous companion does when led by the Spirit can bless *both* individuals in a relationship and up the odds for success.

Another help for Rob—and, equally important, for his wife—was being honest and open about his depression and other mental illnesses. Initially, Rob was prone to hide his difficulties, but eventually he wrote about them, and his stories were published in a local newspaper. And then, one fast Sunday, he stood at the pulpit and shared his struggle with the ward. "Suddenly, everything was easier," Rob says. "People understood. . . . There was an immediate outpouring of love, especially to my wife, and people asking her what they could do to help."

Caregivers need help almost as much as the depressed person does. For Rob's wife, an open line of support from ward members and friends helped relieve some of her burden. According to the National Alliance on Mental Illness (NAMI), "Caregivers who pay attention to their own physical and emotional health are better able to handle the challenges of supporting someone with mental illness. They adapt to changes, build strong relationships and recover from setbacks. The ups and downs in your family member's illness can have a huge impact on you. Improving your relationship with yourself by maintaining your physical and mental health makes you more resilient, helping you weather hard times and enjoy good ones."

Sara Lafkas is a licensed independent clinical social worker (LICSW) in Massachusetts who sometimes works with families of the mentally ill. She echoes NAMI's recommendation for caregivers to nurture themselves and find sources of validation in the struggle:

"Sadness, grief, and helplessness are the feelings most commonly experienced by family members and friends who are caregivers. Wanting the problem to go away, being embarrassed, and feeling hurt—that's all normal. And even though depression and anxiety often have a strong biological component, parents, especially, often feel guilt or self-blame, thinking they have caused the problem or should have done something to prevent it."

Lafkas told me that the siblings of a depressed child may resent the time and attention their parents divert toward the afflicted child. "It's not uncommon that they might even feel fearful: 'Is this going to happen to me?' 'Is this going to play out in my life?'"

And spouses? "They often assume the burdens of extra caretaking and may feel real anger or resentment. It takes a lot of time to support a partner who is suffering. There can be a lack of physical intimacy and feelings of distance or rejection." As Lafkas explained to me, being a caregiver is lonely work: spiritually, emotionally, and physically exhausting.

Michele knows this exhaustion all too well. She is a mother, grandmother, early-morning seminary teacher, and talented interior decorator. She also has a severely depressed spouse. When we spoke, her husband, Robert, was in the throes of his fourth episode with depression—two of which occurred before their marriage. The current episode had been ongoing for six years with no signs of letting up. For Michele, those years have been full of loss. She describes it as: "Robert is 'here' but he's not 'here.' There is such loneliness for me. It's the loss of your companion, the loss of your helpmate, the loss of support, and the huge overwhelming responsibility that then falls on my shoulders to do most everything else needed to run a home and family."

Fortunately, Robert has been able to maintain a job while being depressed, something that many individuals are unable to do. "We've been very blessed that during this episode of depression, his employer has been flexible enough to allow for prolonged periods when he could not go to work. I have not had to support our family financially," Michele says. "I can't even imagine having to try to do that, in addition. I'm abundantly grateful for that. But the weight of everything else falls on me.

"One of the hardest things is that Robert relies on me to receive any and all inspiration for our family and for him." When Robert is depressed, his worst symptoms involve numbness and the complete inability to feel anything—especially the Spirit. He relies on Michele to seek revelation about important family decisions, which have included moves, job changes, and more. The pressure is sometimes frustrating, Michele admits, but "because he receives almost no comfort or guidance from the Spirit—can really not feel it at all—I am hesitant to ever say a negative word about what's happening from my standpoint and my perspective because it just doesn't ever compare to the hell that he's going through. I'm usually pretty quiet about how I'm feeling about my role as a spouse, and that's okay. I can do all these things."

But *how* does she do all these things?

Michele tries to continually maintain an eternal perspective, to regard this as an earthly trial that will eventually be lifted—hopefully in this life and sooner rather than later. She and Robert also talk very openly about his disease. They both understand that it is, indeed, a disease. Robert is a physician, and his medical training informs his perspective, which he shares with his family. One of the serious conversations they have occurs when Robert has suicidal thoughts. He has, in fact, promised Michele and their children that he will not take his own life, no matter how strong the impulse or temptation may be.

MICHELE: "He takes that promise very seriously. . . . He does not want to put that burden on our family. That has taken a little of the worry off my shoulders. It's something that has come to his mind. . . . Mental illness is so painful and what he's dealing with is so painful that there are days when he would just rather be done with his life. He says he wants to get cancer or die in his sleep. He has had times where he's screamed and just said, 'Do you understand that I don't want to be here anymore? It would be easier if I just weren't here.'"

JANE: "What do you say back to him?"

MICHELE: "It's a reality check for me. I think sometimes he feels like I need to understand the severity of it. I can't imagine living with that pain, day in and day out. I wouldn't function if that was my reality. But it's his reality—every day. I tend to be an eternal optimist. I try to help him look for the good and ask, 'Did anything good happen today?'"

JANE: "It must be exhausting."

MICHELE: "There's an amount of pressure and exhaustion. It's taken a little toll on my health. I'm not as healthy as I was six years ago. That's for sure. I have extra weight on me that I'm not particularly thrilled with, but I keep saying, 'When Robert's better, then I can focus on something other than just him.' . . . For the most part, I'm really pretty optimistic, and then there are days when I have a pity party and I'm just irked. You know? There's been a couple of times where I've had strong conversations with God, saying, 'Come on. Can we just let this trial be done?'"

Twice, Michele has received powerful answers from God. They are too sacred to share here, but she says they've given her the wisdom and strength to endure, trusting that the final outcome is that Robert will be healed. She's shared her revelations with Robert, bolstering his hope as well. This is what has most sustained them in this trial: Robert may not be able to *feel* the Spirit for long periods of time, but his testimony is such that he cannot deny the power of a loving God who wants all things to work for our good in the end.

This leads to an interesting juxtaposition. Robert often spends hours a day isolating himself—studying the scriptures, writing in his journal, and praying. He and Michele go to the temple every week although Robert does not feel anything when they attend. He finds no comfort, but, rather than give up, he keeps going, sometimes stubbornly. Michele once reminded him that it's fine not to increase scripture study to two hours a day; one is enough. She had to be firm, telling him: "You are doing absolutely everything, everything in your power to become closer to the Lord. Your scripture study is better than I've ever seen it. It's amazing. You listen to conference talks all the time. You memorize scripture. You don't need to up the ante. This depression is not your fault. Upping this is not going to change it. You're not being punished by the Lord for not doing it enough."

Everything is an art of balance and endurance. Honesty makes us vulnerable, and our vulnerability helps others feel that they are not alone. Sharing the reality of depression from the inside out *and* from the outside in has been critical to Michele and Robert's healthy dialogue about the disease.

Also key is being honest and open with their children about depression and its effect on the dynamics of their family. Fifteen-year-old Sophia acknowledges: "It's especially hard because you have two role models in your life, which are your mom and your dad. And while he still is my role model, it's hard to be able to look up to him when he's feeling this depressed, because you can just tell . . . he's just a totally different person. And it's hard to deal with the fact that this depression is making him act differently."

The fun-loving, communicative, comedic dad Sophia knew in her childhood is not the dad she's known during adolescence. Instead, he's "not as talkative or humorous; he just seems more isolated." But Sophia has inherited her mother's positive attitude and is as determined as Michele to take an eternal perspective when contemplating her dad's suffering. She feels like "the whole family is working together, helping each other through mental illness." Sophia has grown in empathy and understanding for others in adversity and gained an education about the disease itself. "I've learned to be able to see the difference between actual depression and just a sad day," she says. "And I think that's been a really important distinction. I know how depression affects my family's life, and it's not something to joke about. It's a real serious issue that we need to be able to address and be comfortable talking about."

As I spoke with Sophia, I sensed an old soul, with wisdom beyond her years, and so I asked a question that I would have been afraid to face when I was her age.

JANE: "Do you ever worry about having depression yourself?"

SOPHIA: "I was expecting you were going to ask this question. Definitely, I'm worried that I am going to have it, but I'm not worried in the sense that I won't be able to deal with it. . . . I think that's just so comforting to me that if I do happen to develop a mental illness later in my life, I know I'll be able to get through it with the help of my family . . . and the help of the Lord."

THE POWER OF LOVE

Margaret* is a university professor who frequently encounters students who are depressed. But she was also once a fifteen-year-old, like Sophia, with a father who was severely depressed. When her father's struggle first began, he also happened to be president of their stake. It confused her that a man like her father was suffering as he did, because as a child she'd been taught to equate happiness with righteousness and, she assumed, unhappiness with wickedness.

"Especially when I was younger, it was very confusing to me in that I had been taught by teachers and seemingly in the scriptures and life that if you're happy and doing things that are right, then you're living by the Spirit, and if you're dark and sad and not social or whatever else, then you've done something wrong in your life."

She knew intuitively that her father was not unrighteous. His disease, and its effects on him and the family, became a new, precarious

*Name has been changed.

normal. Margaret believed it was her responsibility to make her father happy and felt she'd failed when she couldn't. The self-blame increased when she recognized that some of her siblings also suffered from depression. "With my younger sister, especially, I wanted to open up a door and throw open the windows and give her all the sunshine and tell her funny stories and give her a reason to be smiling and happy. It was hard and frustrating especially in our youth because I felt like I was supposed to be helping her, and I couldn't ever succeed."

She still does this, even though she knows it doesn't work and that she's not at all to blame or responsible for another's depressive state. "It's become a natural tendency to try to create happy moments in their life," she says. "There's also, inside, this fear that they're going to go back down into depression and somehow it's my fault if I'm not on it all the time, if I'm not paying attention to his eyes or her eyes or I'm letting too much loneliness pass by. It's my responsibility."

Growing up in a family led by a father who suffered from depression taught valuable lessons and illustrated ways in which someone can be righteous and a powerful leader while simultaneously coping with a mental illness. One event in particular has stuck with Margaret. Several years ago, she was a young, single adult, living near her parents. On a Sunday morning, on her way to church, Margaret had the impression to stop at her neighbor's house and check in. The neighbor, a single mom of two young kids, didn't answer the door. But Margaret felt like she shouldn't give up. "I opened up the door and called out her name, and she called back to me. I ran in to find her on the kitchen floor. She was suicidal, to say the least, very scared and shaking. She had a bottle of pills in her hand that she was literally in the process of taking and being done." Margaret talked with the woman and convinced her to not do anything until Margaret's dad arrived.

Within minutes, her father was there. He listened to the woman talk about how much better her children's lives would be without her; she couldn't give them the happiness they deserved. She mentioned her thirteen-year-old son specifically. At this point Margaret's father interrupted. "My dad stopped her and held her hands," Margaret said. "I remember him putting his hands to her face and looking at her, and he was so emotional too, which was not typical for my dad to be emotional with someone like that. He was crying and he said to her, 'From the perspective of a thirteen-year-old whose mother committed suicide because of depression and other reasons, I beg of you not to do this thing.' Then he said, 'I know what it's like to be a thirteen-year-old whose mother is depressed. I would rather have a life with a depressed mother who is struggling—any day—than a mother who commits suicide who I never have around for the rest of my life.'"

The moment impressed itself on Margaret, and she watched in silence as her father and this woman embraced and the woman agreed to put away the pills and not take her own life. Her thirteen-year-old son has since served a mission, and the family is doing well. The experience taught Margaret that sometimes the most important thing a person can do to help someone with depression is to hold them and assure them that there are people who love them and want—need—them here, living and breathing, even if it is with depression.

Margaret now uses that tactic to help others. She believes there's nothing better we can do. No words of advice or interventions to fix the problem are as effective as simply offering love.

Carol, whose son, Tim, is a depression sufferer, says, "The whole time he was sick, he didn't want to pray; he lost his testimony. But we required him to have prayer with us in the morning and evening and have scripture study. He fought us every day. He was in a very dark place. We just had to love him and pray that we'd say the right things. Pray for ourselves. Imagine in our minds a healthier time and place. We would continually tell him, 'You're doing the best you can and we love you. You're accepted and it's okay and we'll be here for you for whatever you need.'

"After he got better, he thanked us—it gave him a lifeline. He is so faithful in his calling now. He feels like he's been saved from death and he wants to give back to the Lord."

Love works because it is hopeful. It illuminates the possibility of a joyful future. Trying to "fix" a depressed person fails because fixing, by its very nature, is nonaccepting; it implies an innate wrongness with the person. One husband graciously opened his journal to share what he'd learned from trying to "fix" his wife's problems. "Men in general," he wrote, "and especially husbands, are natural fixers. It's in our DNA. When we are told about something being wrong or broken, our minds and efforts point immediately to finding the solution. This works great for household repairs, but when we're confronted with emotional problems, this approach can be frustrating for both the person with the mental-health challenge and the spouse too focused on trying to 'just fix it.'"

Telling a depressed person that things "aren't as bad as they think they are," urging them to lose themselves in church work or other service, reminding them of the power of prayer; all are as counterproductive to healing as shaming or threatening would be. As this husband wrote in his journal, "What I now know to be true is that I should start from a place of trying to understand her emotions. Feelings expressed are opportunities to connect rather than puzzles requiring a solution. My job became to simply love her, tell her so, and tell her why. It doesn't 'fix' her depression, but that was never the goal. What it does do is make her mental health a thing that both of us can work through instead of some mess that needs to be cleaned up or put away."

Their new approach might be a long way from an ideal storybook tale—but most marriages are, and, for that matter, so are most things in life. Other people's marriages, families, and lives are never as simple or as perfect as we perceive them to be. We marry for better or for worse. When we have children, we take them as they come. It's easy to judge or to be jealous, but it's godly to seek understanding, love unconditionally, and do the hard work demanded by daily life in this world.

Another husband told me: "When we're dealing with people who have mental illness and we can't understand, I think we need to seek our own inspiration. We need to seek to change our own attitudes and thought patterns because we need to have the humility to understand that maybe the way we see the world and the way we experience it is not the one and only way to see it and experience it. Seeking the Spirit, loving with a Christlike love—I think that's what helps the suffering person feel the love that *we* have for them, and also the love that the *Lord* has for them."

The circle of family can expand to include a loving ward and Church family, with members who often want to help but hesitate because their understanding and experience are limited. But really, in most cases, being helpful isn't complex. Just being there can make all the difference in the world. Virginia Pearce told me how her feelings about those who are less active changed when she served in Relief Society. She found that many of those sisters who didn't attend had strong testimonies and a desire to keep growing in the gospel, but they also struggled with a variety of emotional illnesses, such as social anxiety, depression, obsessive-compulsive disorder, and others. These illnesses made Church callings next to impossible and even church attendance difficult.

"Somehow," she said, "we've got to bring church to them." Many were unable to feel God's love. "One of my friends," she told me, "was in and out of the hospital with terrible postpartum depression. When she was in the hospital down to nothing she said, 'I couldn't feel Him. I couldn't feel any hope; it was like a dead tree that had been cut off, but I knew the roots were there and at some point some life would come back.' I think that's a really good picture: you have to believe that in the roots, even though nothing is growing on top, there's life down there and it is the Savior. It's the Savior."

What can you do when you know someone who is in that condition? "We just keep bumping into them with our light," Sister Pearce says. "Don't take your light away from them; don't distance yourself from them. It doesn't mean you have to preach to them or get them to come to church or find a way to fix them. Trust that just your presence in their lives makes a difference because you are full of light and love—and that's what we all long for. It's one of the reasons we gather on Sundays—to feel nourished by His light and love. Just your presence matters. A lot."

I love the story my friend shared about her brother, Ryan, who suffered from depression his entire adult life.

"One year Ryan helped me install an underground sprinkler system for a new garden. When we finished it and tried it out, it blew some connection at the meter, causing a huge geyser of water. It took days to figure out and repair the problem, and we had to shut off water to the house again and again. Ultimately Ryan dug a hole almost six feet deep to get a clear view of the whole connection area (this was in Utah where freezing temps require water pipes to be buried down a ways). Ryan, who was at most five foot eight, spent hours at the bottom of this hole with the top of his head just above ground level. He named it 'The Pit of Despair.'

"One night, tired of being without water in the house, my husband and I took our kids and went to a late movie. It was nearly midnight when we got home, and as we approached the house we could see Ryan in our headlights, down in the pit. His wife, whose name is

Charity—no joke—was standing by him at ground level, shining a light down on him."

The takeaway: some among us spend a lot of time in midnight blackness at the bottom of a pit of despair. They need charity to shine the Light on them.

CHAPTER 10

The Lower Lights:
A Stewardship of
Help and Hope

We then that are strong ought to bear the infirmities
of the weak, and not to please ourselves.

—Romans 15:1

As he sat on the stand Sunday after Sunday, a shepherd watching over his flock, Bishop Frank Gentile became well acquainted with the prevalent and debilitating nature of mental illness. Here's a snapshot of what he encountered during five years of service in his Massachusetts ward: twenty members with clinical depression, seven with serious eating disorders, five with attention-deficit/hyperactivity disorder, four with bipolar disorder, four with post-traumatic stress disorder, three with obsessive-compulsive disorder, three with serious anxiety/social phobia disorders, two with borderline personality disorder, one with schizophrenia, one with multiple-personality disorder, five suicide attempts, including youth, and one suicide. This daunting list doesn't include those with serious addictions to things like alcohol, drugs, and pornography.

A TYPICAL CONGREGATION

This case may seem extreme, but it's not; the numbers jibe with national statistics. In any given year, approximately one in five adults in the United States experiences mental illness. Approximately one in five active members (including adults and children) of Bishop Gentile's ward was stricken with some form of mental illness. This included some of the "strongest" members of the ward—his wife and son among them, as well as members of the ward council, a counselor in the stake presidency, and the Relief Society president's children.

Fortunately, Bishop Gentile was already familiar with mental illness because of his wife's and son's difficulties and was thus well equipped to help his members who struggled.

"There is a lot of variability in the level of Church leadership experience in this area," Bishop Gentile says. "And so I look back at my time as a bishop and realize how lucky I was because I had a lot of experience in my own family. I knew a lot about alcoholism, I knew a lot about bipolar, I knew a lot about depression. And since I work in biotech, I knew a lot about these drugs—what they are, what they do, what they don't do, what they target, and what they don't target."

But what about Church leaders who don't have the background Gentile does? What about the bishop who has never encountered depression or obsessive-compulsive disorder? Or the stake president who unknowingly preaches some of the myths of mental illness? Or the Relief Society president unfamiliar with the warning signs of depression or suicide when they manifest in a sister under her stewardship?

On the whole, leaders of most faiths—including ours—are unlikely to have a great deal of experience, much less expertise, in dealing with mental-health issues. A study by Baylor University psychologists found that churches are surprisingly likely to overlook the needs of congregants who suffer from mental illness. "Faith communities fail to adequately engage . . . because they lack awareness of the issues and understanding of the important ways they can help," said Dr. Diana Garland, dean of Baylor's School of Social Work and a coauthor of the study.

As Andrew Solomon wrote in *The Noonday Demon*, depression's victims roll through their "lives in invisible wheelchairs, dressed in invisible body casts."

So what can the Church—and we, specifically, as its members—do for those who are struck with these invisible illnesses, depression in particular? Exactly the same things we do so well for people who are confined to visible wheelchairs and body casts, and what we do for the indigent, the lonely, and the bereft. We can withhold judgment and extend a helping hand. Sometimes we assume that the sheep we should seek are those lost to sin or inactivity or addiction, but, in fact, many are lost in the dark wilderness of depression.

Ministering can help Churchwide on a number of levels. Individual Church members, who covenant at baptism to mourn with and comfort others, can always become better informed about mental illness and engage the embattled with empathy. Local leaders of wards and stakes can receive and provide improved training to recognize victims of mental illness and guide them to appropriate resources. Stakes and wider regions of the Church can create mental-health-focused task forces to both raise awareness and combat crises among their members. At every level, more first-person stories and simple acknowledgment of mental-health issues can illuminate the topic and reassure sufferers and their loved ones that they are not alone.

It is not a stretch to say that we, as individual members of The Church of Jesus Christ of Latter-day Saints, are under obligation to seek out the sick and the suffering and to come to their aid. We've been given this mandate in scripture after scripture, talk after talk:

" . . . bear one another's burdens, that they may be light; . . . mourn with those that mourn; . . . comfort those that stand in need of comfort" (Mosiah 18:8–9).

" . . . when ye are in the service of your fellow beings ye are only in the service of your God" (Mosiah 2:17).

" . . . if ye have not charity, ye are nothing. . . . But charity is the pure love of Christ, . . . and whoso is found possessed of it at the last day, it shall be well with him" (Moroni 7:46–47).

" . . . love one another; as I have loved you" (John 13:34).

"The Savior is telling us that unless we lose ourselves in service to others, there is little purpose to our own lives" (Thomas S. Monson).

"Let our hearts and hands be stretched out in compassion toward others, for everyone is walking his or her own difficult path. As disciples of Jesus Christ, our Master, we are called to support and heal rather than condemn" (Dieter F. Uchtdorf).

With empathy and love as our objectives, we can answer these calls to help. How? This chapter is an attempt to provide some ideas. First among them is a call to learn about the stigma and myths surrounding depression and be willing to talk about them openly. Part of that call to action is a plea to let go of those same myths and stigma as we love and minister to those we find who are suffering.

OVERTURNING THE HARMFUL MYTHS OF MENTAL ILLNESS

Elder Alexander B. Morrison, an emeritus member of the First Quorum of the Seventy, has written and spoken frequently about mental illness. As an internationally respected scientist, he taught with both authority and knowledge. As a parent of a mentally ill child, he spoke with empathy and experience. "Among the most painful trials an individual or family can face is that of mental illness," he wrote in an *Ensign* article he penned on the topic. "By mental illness I do not mean the temporary social and emotional concerns experienced as part of the normal wear and tear of living. Rather, I mean a disorder that causes mild to severe disturbances in thinking and behavior. If such disturbances are sufficiently severe and of sufficient duration, they may significantly impair a person's ability to cope with life's ordinary demands. These illnesses may even threaten life itself, as in severe depression, or be so debilitating that the sufferer is unable to function effectively."

Elder Morrison outlined several myths about mental illness in the article, including the misconceptions that "All mental illness is caused by sin," "Mentally ill persons just lack willpower," and "All that people with mental illness need is a priesthood blessing." His insightful article is a must-read for those dealing with the challenges of mental illness.

Ryan Thompson is both a medical doctor and a former bishop with experience counseling people who are depressed. He says: "I think it can be damaging or risky to somebody if they approach mental illness in a way that does not pull together the best of religion and the best of science. . . . If somebody solely relies on a spiritual approach to treating depression, I think they're less likely to be successful. . . . I also think that if somebody solely relies on the physical component of treating depression, they might be missing out on some potential spiritual parts of it that they need to be addressing in their lives."

Dr. Thompson often uses an analogy when he talks to individuals about the need to get help, as well as the sometimes-long recovery process. A depressed person is like a pool of cold water, he says. To warm a pool of water, you don't pour in cups of hot water one by one; you use heaters. Still, it takes time. Heaters are analogous to all the different methods of *physical* care available: cognitive behavioral therapy, medication, and proper sleep, fitness, and nutrition regimens.

The sun also helps heat the pool. But although it is ever present, sometimes there's cloud cover and the darkness of night. This is analogous to the Savior, the Son of God. Sometimes the cloud cover of depression is too thick and blocks the comfort of the Spirit; but the Spirit is still ever present, and there are many spiritual things that can be done in tandem with the physical to help speed up the recovery process: prayer, scripture study, service, and so on.

"Changing the course of a mental illness, like changing the temperature of a large pool of water, takes time," Thompson says. "You can't just take a medicine. They work and they *do* help, like heaters do warm the water; but you may not reach your potential if you don't also learn how to redirect your thoughts and form better ways of going about life by drawing upon the power of the Son."

MEETING THE NEED BY
RECOGNIZING THE NEEDY

Knowing that each of our Latter-day Saint wards is likely home to dozens of Saints with depression, anxiety, and other illnesses is one thing; knowing *who* those members are is something else entirely. Once you know the myths surrounding depression, the next steps are to become well versed in the signs and symptoms of mental illness, acknowledge the reality of their biological component, and share awareness of professional counseling and medical therapy. This is something every member of a ward can do, from the bishop to Primary teachers to quorum and class members.

Warning signs of depression and other mental illnesses include prolonged sadness, loss of interest or pleasure, feelings of worthlessness, disturbed sleep patterns, change in weight or appetite, loss of will to live, excessive worrying or fear, and loss of concentration.

While a bishop, Frank Gentile found that watching for symptoms of mental illness in his members was a no-brainer. "Sometimes it was obvious—there'd be a big change in their weight or their hygiene," he says. "Or somebody who was never, ever missing in action in a calling somehow started becoming a no-show."

We can all watch for changes in church attendance. We can proactively identify an isolated teen. We can notice the new mother struggling to cope with her responsibilities. If something seems like it's not quite right, there's probably a reason.

When Cynthia Pierce became stake Relief Society president in the Nashua New Hampshire Stake, she already had personal experience dealing with depression and other mental illnesses with some of her own children. In fact, her seventeen-year-old son died by suicide while she was serving. Cynthia dove into her calling with tremendous compassion and empathy for the sisters she served.

"As I traveled the stake and listened to ward Relief Society presidents and bishops, the number-one challenge they're facing is mental health," Cynthia says. "When you get to the bottom of it, a lot of the welfare cases, a lot of the unemployment cases, a lot of the problems facing dysfunctional families are driven by underlying mental-health problems."

For Cynthia, knowing what mental illness looks like—and recognizing its symptoms—opened a door of insight into many of her sisters' burdens.

Others, though, must learn to recognize the symptoms before they can gain insight into the struggles of those who are depressed. Dan Ellertson, a former bishop of a Salt Lake City singles ward, says he didn't have a clue what to look for until his own son returned early from his mission due to depression. Witnessing firsthand the genuine pain and incapacity caused by mental illness and the stinging stigma that accompanies it, Ellertson learned what to watch for and then armed himself to aid the members of his ward.

"Without my experience with my son, I would have been like any other bishop," Bishop Ellertson says. "The best training we're given is, 'Okay, call LDS Family Services.' But the more bishops understand, the more bishops are in a position to not react negatively or ignorantly to any situation a ward member brings to them, and the better off we'll all be."

Bishop Gentile found it helpful to use his personal experience and familiarity with mental illness as a way to speak frankly about it.

This method of personal story sharing allowed many in his congregation to feel more comfortable acknowledging the need for help.

"If I had somebody come into my office to talk to me, and it was clear to me that they were having some sort of mental-health issue, I would bluntly talk to them about it—I would just say, 'Have you ever been treated for depression? Do you have depression in your family?'" Bishop Gentile says. "Sometimes I'd ask open-ended questions: 'How's your sleep? Do you feel anxious a lot? Are you worried about a lot of things?'"

Usually, he says, that was enough to get people to realize that there was a real problem going on. From there, he could refer them to a doctor or therapist—or both.

Bishop Ellertson advises bishops and other leaders to—above all else—make it clear that when members of the Church speak with a spiritual leader, they'll be listened to.

"The best that bishops can do is be open and approachable and understanding and soft and sympathetic and encouraging and patient, because that's the bishop's role," he says. "This can show in your body language, your sympathy, your understanding, your follow-on questions of wanting to understand more, and not judging the situation. When a person goes in to talk to the bishop, they need to know they're going to be listened to; they need to know they're going to be understood. You always leave the door open and leave the channels of communication open, and let them know they have an advocate. Bishops are advocates just like the Savior is our advocate."

And that attitude Bishop Ellertson describes—one of openness and approachability and understanding and sympathy—can extend to all members of the Church community. Dr. Rob Waller, a consultant psychiatrist for the UK's National Health Service, has studied the effects of mental-health issues in Christian circles. For him, the empathetic response of church leaders *and* church members is fundamental.

"Some people have been told that they ought to pray more, to snap out of it, or that they just need more faith," he told *Christianity Today*. "But what they actually need is a healing and accepting community. I was shocked how little the church talked about these problems. The church needs to foster a culture that means that this topic can be discussed if it needs to be. They need to be clear that they are mental-health friendly."

A skill all of us in a "healing and accepting community" could practice and implement is that of empathy. A little bit of empathy goes a long way, as Jenifer describes in this experience from more than three decades ago:

"The first experience I had at BYU, I was really, really depressed. It was the first time I'd ever experienced anything like that. I actually went into the Wilkinson Center and I climbed under a table. I just crawled, held my knees; I knew that I was being weird. This was not normal, but I just didn't know what else to do. A student came over and she said, 'Can I talk to you?' She brought me into a classroom and . . . she just had this love and compassion. I felt like she was this little guardian angel of sorts, even though I never saw her again.

"There's one thing that I remember that she said, and it has stayed with me for thirty some odd years. She said, 'Life is a process.'

"After that, I just felt like I could have empathy for anyone. You never know what's going on in someone's life. I know that may sound trite, but when a person is depressed, you really can't see anything on the outside."

SHARING STORIES OF SUCCESS

Earlier chapters have provided examples of priesthood leaders acting to aid depression sufferers: Apostles urging a stake president to delegate duties to his counselors so that he can rest and heal from his emotional illness; a wise bishop extending a quiet but useful calling to a struggling brother; inspired mission presidents adapting mission rules and environments to help afflicted young people serve in meaningful ways. These are stories of successful ministering that we need to share and learn from.

For a few years, Bishop Gentile shared a message, accompanied by a PowerPoint presentation full of useful information on mental illness, throughout his stake—in third-hour Sunday lessons, Young Men and Young Women classes, and ward councils. He has used his personal experiences with mental illness as a tool to relate to those who are struggling.

"I think there's a lot of weight that can be given to first-person stories," he says. "It's when people share stories in this area that I think real understanding comes. When I could share those first-person stories with people, I had more success in reaching them, developing a relationship, and getting them the help that they needed. Or getting them to recognize that, in fact, they needed to get some help, or they needed to see a counselor, or a therapist, or a physician."

Bishop Gentile's presentations cover everything from the prevalence of mental illness to myths and misconceptions within the Church to a case study on suicide. The messages of empathy, compassion, and the role of the Savior's Atonement are always front and center.

"The more we talk about it, the more we raise awareness," he says. "I can tell you that when I go to a third-hour lesson in one of our units and give a presentation on this, I get a lot of nodding heads. Occasionally people open up about their own issues, or issues within their families. And the people next to them don't know anything about it. They're in their ward, and they may have known them for years. But they don't know this about them."

In my own area of New England, a local stake is taking "mental-health friendliness" to a new level. The Nashua New Hampshire Stake has developed a formal initiative in the form of a wellness committee (something of a subcommittee to the stake welfare committee) with a broad focus to help the poor and needy—and a specific bull's-eye on mental health. Dubbed by the stake president as the M25 Committee, the group uses chapter 25 of the book of Matthew as its inspiration:

"Then shall the righteous answer him, saying, Lord, when saw we thee an hungred, and fed thee? or thirsty, and gave thee drink?

"When saw we thee a stranger, and took thee in? or naked, and clothed thee?

"Or when saw we thee sick, or in prison, and came unto thee?

"And the King shall answer and say unto them, Verily I say unto you, Inasmuch as ye have done it unto one of the least of these my brethren, ye have done it unto me" (Matthew 25:37–40).

The M25 Committee aims to be a resource regarding all things mental health, addictions, employment, and welfare. More specifically, the committee helps connect local Church leaders—bishops, Relief Society presidents, and others—to members of the stake who have specialized knowledge or personal experience in various aspects of mental-health care.

"Most bishops have times when they just don't know what they can do," says Franz Busse, a high councilor in the stake who helped establish the M25 program. "This committee was created as an attempt to provide some sort of resource to help the different bishops and ward councils with the complex emergencies that happen on these personal levels."

Let's imagine a new bishop has just learned about a young mother in his ward who seems to be facing severe depression. This good bishop is well equipped to provide love and compassion and a listening ear, but he's not so sure what to do beyond recommending she get in touch with LDS Family Services. That's where M25 comes in.

For starters, the committee has—vetted and ready—a directory of all the applicable state resources, agencies, nonprofits, and NGOs in the area that the bishop might need to call or pass on to the ward member.

Next, the committee acts as a council, offering a level of subject matter expertise well beyond what a traditional ward council can provide. Committee members, who meet together every other month and communicate frequently in between meetings, have received training on relevant topics to add to their experience and familiarity with these wellness-related issues.

The committee can recommend therapists, physicians, psychiatrists, and psychotherapists who have previously interacted with other members in the stake. Positive experiences with mental-health professionals reported to the M25 task force help to build a catalog of vetted experts. When a child has an anxiety disorder, parents can reach out to M25 for a list of well-researched healthcare providers instead of calling the thirty providers accepted by their insurance and hoping one of them is both available *and* a good match.

Most important, the wellness committee is there to provide aid along every step of a family's difficult journey with mental illness.

"Sometimes, when people are trying to do this on their own, they give up and quit trying," Cynthia Pierce says. "But having a wellness committee to carry them through the process, to help them work through the ins and outs of their insurance, to help them find a counselor who will be a good fit. . . . It's comforting to know you have somebody on your team who's going to stay with the process until you have all the support needed to move forward."

The M25 program is in its infancy, but the group has already engaged in critical dialogues that were once avoided and stigmatized.

"When I was a ward Relief Society president, I remember the stake Relief Society president asking me to talk to the sisters in the ward and see if there were counselors they had used who understood our faith so they could compile a list for others," Cynthia Pierce says. "But there are a lot of roadblocks to that approach. People are reluctant to admit they're in counseling. They want privacy. Many times they are reluctant to come forward and share who they're using as a counselor."

But as the committee has elevated the profile of its mission—through training sessions with bishops and ward councils, lessons to the youth, and presentations to entire congregations—progress has come.

Sister Pierce illustrates the advantages of this collaborative approach: "There was a recently reactivated single sister in our ward. She has a son who was attacked on the street and basically left for dead when he was about eighteen. He survived but has all kinds of mental-health challenges as a result. While I was ward Relief Society president, we supported her the best way we knew how by providing listening ears and love and occasionally helping with things like food orders or service in the home. Then a new sister moved into the ward and helped us recognize that the woman's son qualified for disability and all kinds of state services. She immediately connected this mother with government resources that have helped with his care, both mentally and physically, and also helped her financially. The whole situation was sitting right under my nose the entire time I was Relief Society president, but I had no idea how to connect her with the substantial support she needed until someone with more experience got involved."

THE LOWER LIGHTS

Elder Jeffrey R. Holland's 2013 general conference talk on mental health was a watershed moment for both Latter-day Saints who battle depression and those who love them. To hear an Apostle of the Lord speak to this long-taboo issue—and admit his own struggle with it!—kindled hope in many sinking hearts. I have quoted him repeatedly for this reason; none of us can feel encouraged and understood *too much,* after all. Elder Morrison, President Ballard, and other General Authorities have offered comfort and wisdom on this and related subjects. They understand the widespread and complex nature of this adversity—and they speak on behalf of a loving Lord who has descended below all things, including the depths of depressive illness.

Indeed, the Savior knows the trials and travails of this hard passage. He desires to succor those weary souls who travel it, encompassing them in His love and light. And we are His torchbearers! As leaders of Church units, as priesthood quorum or auxiliary members, and as neighbors and friends, we each play a part in carrying the Lord's light to those left behind in life's dark places.

Let me bring to your remembrance one of the great stories in Latter-day Saint history. It is one that also happens to be part of my own family history, and so I hold it dear to my heart. It involves the rescue of the Willie and Martin handcart companies. More than once I have thrilled to this piece of our communal lore, recounted at the pulpit by apostles and prophets. And yet, I think no matter how many times I hear it told, it is impossible to truly understand the hardship, the hopelessness, the fearful desperation and isolation felt by our brothers and sisters who were stranded on the plains. Brigham Young, apprised by messengers of the dire circumstances, issued a call to action during the general conference that was convened at that time:

"Many of our brethren and sisters are on the plains with handcarts, and probably many are now seven hundred miles from this place, and they must be brought here, we must send assistance to them," the prophet told the congregation.

"That is my religion; that is the dictation of the Holy Ghost that I possess. It is to save the people.

"I shall call upon the Bishops this day. I shall not wait until to-morrow, nor until the next day. . . .

"I will tell you all that your faith, religion, and profession of religion, will never save one soul of you in the Celestial Kingdom of our God, unless you carry out just such principles as I am now teaching you. *Go and bring in those people now on the plains.*"

In the handwritten notes of my grandmother Beulah Clayson's history, I have read: "I am proud to be able to say that three of my great-grandfathers, Daniel Thompson, William Robins and James William Adams, were among those young men, who, with their teams went east to help bring the Saints who were stranded on the plains to Utah. Marvelous is the work of those who have gone before us, tremendous is our responsibility, sobering is our acceptance of their suffering, example, commitment and dedication. Have we the humility, courage and devotion to accept their offering and magnify our responsibilities?"

President Gordon B. Hinckley, who often referenced this episode, once echoed my grandmother's sentiments, saying, "I am grateful that those days of pioneering are behind us. I am thankful that we do not have brethren and sisters stranded in the snow, freezing and dying, while trying to get to this, their Zion in the mountains. But there are people, not a few, whose circumstances are desperate and who cry out for help and relief."

Among those who feel the most desperate, I believe, are those who suffer from mental illness. It is our privilege—and the essence of our discipleship—to bring them in. Because there is no cure for depression, we cannot rescue them in a way that heals them of their illness, but we can save them from being stranded alone in the winter of their pain.

I hope that we will begin to speak more freely about depression, that individuals will feel able to share their stories and their pain without fear of judgment and with confidence that help will be forthcoming. I hope the conversation will also include an open sharing of "best practices": the accumulating wisdom of a worldwide congregation in which every member is a lay minister of some sort, an undershepherd of the Good Shepherd whose Church it is. I hope we will bring the dialogue about depression out of the shadows and into the light, becoming more effective stewards of each other in the process.

I love the inspiring old hymn "Brightly Beams Our Father's Mercy":

> *Brightly beams our Father's mercy*
> *From his lighthouse evermore,*
> *But to us he gives the keeping*
> *Of the lights along the shore. . . .*
> *Trim your feeble lamp, my brother;*
> *Some poor sailor, tempest-tossed,*
> *Trying now to make the harbor,*
> *In the darkness may be lost.*

It is one of the miracles of the gospel and the restored Church that none of us has to solve these thorny problems all alone. The Lord is the light and the Savior of our souls. We are simply asked to help each other see His light and find His salvation. For one who is adrift in the fog of depression, with the Lord's lighthouse grown dim or lost to view, that is valuable service indeed. Whether the torch we carry casts 10,000 lumens or only one, it is our willingness to take a place among the lower lights that will make the difference.

CHAPTER 11

"The Most Powerful Medicine on Earth"

Open your mouths and spare not, and you shall be laden
with sheaves upon your backs, for lo, I am with you.

—Doctrine and Covenants 33:9

As I neared the end of the writing process for this book, I was asked to present a fireside on the topic to my home stake in Cambridge, Massachusetts. Because I've had the opportunity to give a fair number of talks and presentations over the years, I was surprised at how anxious I felt in the weeks leading up to the fireside. I knew that I needed to—wanted to—share my own journey through depression, which was what prompted this project in the first place. But it would be a very public declaration in front of people with whom I would interact for years to come, and it made me nervous.

Was I really prepared for this? What would people think? Would their opinions about me change? Why did I even care about that? I felt very exposed and, frankly, vulnerable. Several times I woke in the middle of the night wondering and worrying what would happen after I shared this part of me. Somehow, it felt much more real than writing down the words on paper ever had.

Thankfully, the evening came and went, and I survived! As far as I know, no one thinks any less of me now. But even if they do, it won't change how I feel now about sharing my story. And that is this: sharing stories about depression is the best, first step in fighting both the disease itself and the stigma that surrounds it.

It bears repeating this quote from chapter 2: "Telling your story—while being witnessed with loving attention by others who care—*may be the most powerful medicine on earth.*" I believe, in fact, that sharing is *vital* to lightening burdens and healing broken minds. I have witnessed this in others and experienced it for myself when people I didn't know learned that I was writing this book and called me out of the blue to share their stories with me. That sharing of experiences, of things we have learned that can help—as well as what we suspect can harm—shifts some of the weight from the shoulders of the afflicted to the shoulders of those who are more able to encourage, support, or even just sit in the gloom with us. As we share like this, we build a community where everyone feels safe enough to tell his or her story and where we can stand as witnesses to each other that "the Lord God [does visit His] people in their afflictions" (Mosiah 24:14).

Of all the people with whom I could share my story, then, who better than my fellow sojourners in The Church of Jesus Christ of Latter-day Saints—those who have covenanted to "mourn with those that mourn; yea, and comfort those that stand in need of comfort" (Mosiah 18:9)? I believe Elder Holland knew this when he spoke about mental illness in general conference. I definitely know it now. And so do the many brave souls who willingly shared their own depression stories with me for this book.

Seth shared with me one of my now-favorite quotes: "Depression thrives in secrecy but shrinks in empathy."

And my friend Heather wrote to me: "The thing I come back to again and again is how we are doomed to suffer without support; we are just isolated in our troubles if we cannot share. Everyone who is suffering—with depression, with a spouse or child with depression, whatever—needs people to share with. And we're out here. There are enough of us that have experienced it, that understand it. It's true that there is stigma, but it is not universal. There are caring people who want to help and who have the experience to empathize. There are still those who judge, but fewer all the time. . . . Depression sufferers need to share; they need to trust enough to open up, and they will find in every congregation there are true disciples who will accept them and help them. . . . When left all alone we are in real trouble."

After I gave my presentation at the fireside that Sunday evening, I received a wonderful email from a sister in my stake whom I didn't know but who had been in the audience. She had dealt with depression on and off for years but had always kept very quiet about it, worrying constantly that there would be harsh consequences if someone knew she wasn't the highly functioning, put-together person everyone thought she was. We exchanged messages, shared more of our stories with one another, met for lunch, and each gained a new friend to help lighten our burdens. In one of her messages, she wrote:

"When your faith is such a huge part of your life and your life feels broken, one of the first places you look to fix is your faith. I think about the famous Gordon B. Hinckley quote, 'Bring what good you have and see if we can't add to it,' and want to spin it to say, 'Bring what heartache and problems you have and see if we can't try to understand them.' Because at the end of the day, connections are made from feeling understood, right?"

Of course, she is right. Sharing, carrying others' burdens, sitting in silence beside a friend as we listen to her talk about depression—these are all things the Savior would do if He were here.

Recently, my family and I took a trip to India, where we had the opportunity to meet, serve, and love people who are burdened with the curse of leprosy. I look back at those weeks frequently and find myself thinking often about the Savior and His association with the men and women who suffered with leprosy in His time. Jesus didn't heal them by avoiding them. He waded right into the mess with His help and with His hope. Leprosy is a disease that can't be hidden—people are literally, physically falling apart. Mental health needs to be like that; it needs to be dragged into the light of day where we can see that people are falling apart and where those who are willing to wade in and help can do so.

Who cares if there are bystanders and finger pointers? There always have been and always will be. We aren't going to solve that problem. But people who will brave the challenge to make their struggles known—and who will reject the notion that they should be ashamed—are an important first step to us becoming an honest and supportive Church community.

In each person I interviewed, I saw pain, vulnerability, and loneliness, but I also saw love and hope and life. I heard stories about Christ's Atonement at work, stories of rescue, stories of finding sustenance in a wilderness of shadows and stone. As people told their stories—as I told my story—depression was given a face. Those faces became imprinted on my heart, and I now carry them with me and let them buoy me. They have changed my life.

The experience of this book has given me tremendous compassion and empathy. I can spot immediately those around me who have that "look"—the look of hopelessness that comes when you're feeling absolutely nothing, when you would just rather slip away. And I truly believe that once you have suffered, you have a particular responsibility to show greater love and empathy for others who suffer as well, and a greater responsibility to share your story so that others may know they are not alone. And, perhaps, to leave a record of your resilience and survival.

Andrew Solomon, in *The Noonday Demon,* writes: "By seeing how many kinds of resilience and strength and imagination are to be found, one can appreciate not only the horror of depression but also the complexity of human vitality. . . . All of us have stories, and the true survivors have compelling stories."

I believe that healing for those who suffer from depression begins when we listen to these stories, when we encourage those who tell them to speak out about their pain and share their vulnerability. It comes, too, when we are willing to be vulnerable along with them, to sit with them in their pain and, hopefully, draw them out of isolation. Each person I interviewed, and nearly every book and article I picked up on the topic, agreed that "depression will only intensify in the private cocoon we spin at our lowest."

My wish is for you to find the hope that is entwined with the sorrow in every story in this book. They are stories of survival and, above all, stories of faith in a God who loves us and has not left us alone. Elder Alexander B. Morrison, in writing about mental illness, reminds us to "recognize that the fire of affliction, which scars and diminishes some souls, purifies and ennobles others, transforming them into celestial creatures filled with supernal joy.

"Never forget: 'All your losses will be made up to you in the resurrection, provided you continue faithful. By the vision of the Almighty I have seen it,' said the Prophet Joseph Smith, who knew more about anguish, disappointment, and spiritual affliction than most."

I never thought I would say it, but I am grateful for this journey of depression, and especially for these last two years, during which I became privy to the shared stories of so many remarkable, brave, resilient, compassionate, and merciful people I met along the way. God lives and loves us. He has offered His Beloved Son, Jesus Christ, to be our Savior. And it is not only ultimate salvation of which we speak: Jesus is saving us every day. He has borne our sorrows. He visits us in our afflictions. We are privileged to be His ministers. This I know now more than ever.

ACKNOWLEDGMENTS

This book was a labor of love, but I did not labor alone.

Deepest gratitude goes to my dear friend Janna DeVore for her help during the writing process. This book wouldn't have happened without her. She brought compassion to these pages and spent countless hours helping me get the stories just right. It was my great honor to be partners on this journey. Thank you, Janna, from the bottom of my heart.

Many thanks to Heather Hunt, who restored order to this project early on by single-handedly organizing thousands of pages of documents in a massive iCloud file. She is a brilliant editor and beautiful writer, and her generosity of spirit was an unexpected gift in the process of finishing this work. I am profoundly grateful to you, Heather.

During my early "I-can't-possibly-do-this-where-do-I-even-start" moments, my husband's writing partner, Arthur Goldwag, twice volunteered to drive to Boston from his home in Brooklyn, New York, to help me outline and structure this book. During those intense, day-long sessions, he kept saying to me, "Yes, you *can* do this!" and because of his confidence, I started to believe it.

I am deeply indebted to Louise Jorgensen, PhD, from the Association of Mormon Counselors and Psychotherapists, Kris Doty-Yells, PhD, and Dr. Jacqueline Olds, who enthusiastically shared treasure troves of research—their presentations, slides, books, references— anything I asked for. They offered critical guidance and insight throughout the research and writing process, as well as invaluable suggestions after reading drafts of the manuscript. Without their help, I was at the mercy of my own inadequate devices.

Many thanks to other mental-health professionals who generously shared their time and expertise: Dr. Esther Dechant, Mindy Soloman, PhD, and Dr. Jennifer Hagman. Their wisdom and empathy have informed the writing, enlightened me personally, and helped to shape a final book that is much enriched by their contributions.

Thank you also to my team at Deseret Book, especially Jana Erickson, who for years occasionally nudged me toward another book project and was immediately supportive when I called her out of the blue to pitch this one. She came out of retirement three years later to deliver the completed manuscript to Deseret Book. My friend, Laurel Christensen Day, shepherded this project through its final stages and always seemed to reply to my emails within minutes. You are truly the best. I was blessed to have the assistance of Emily Watts, who edited the manuscript with surgical precision and, most importantly, with deep respect for the stories and content.

I am likewise grateful to the people who shaped this book after reading drafts of the manuscript: Kristiina Sorensen, Erin Gentile, Jim MacArthur, PhD, and Sara Lafkas, LICSW. Special thanks are due to Robert Millet, who offered pages of insightful feedback and doctrinal direction. My heartfelt thanks also to Jessie Hawkes, Ashley Dickson, Bob Brown, Alex Wu, and Whitney Johnson; I am so grateful for your help and encouragement along the way. To Janice Evans, mentor and friend for twenty-five years, who taught me early in my career to write and document my journeys, wherever they led. And to Karen Shiffman, Belle Liang, and Julie Marriott—every girl should have kind, supportive friends like you have been to me.

Thanks to my sister, Hannah Smith, whose brainstorm of ideas on a family vacation several summers ago evolved into the book's early chapters. Her mind is a wonder to me. And to my parents—my greatest examples—who always taught us to do good and be good.

Much love and thanksgiving to my children; you are my deepest source of joy and my most compelling motivation for writing this book.

I could never express enough gratitude to my husband, Mark. At the height of this project, my files, books, and interview notes occupied nearly every room of the house. He didn't grumble when I hijacked the dining-room table and made it my workspace for months at a time. He supported the professional transcription of thousands of pages of interviews—and otherwise encouraged me—endlessly. Mark is the genuine and gentle soul at the heart of all that's good in our family.

Most of all, I am grateful to all the people who shared their stories; I am humbled by your trust and confidence in me. Your honesty and authenticity have created a wellspring of inspiration that I will drink from for the rest of my life.

Jane Clayson Johnson
Belmont, Massachusetts

ENDNOTES

All quotes not cited here are from personal interviews with the author.

CHAPTER 1
DEPRESSION IN THE FIRST PERSON: MY STORY

Page 3, "I am now the most miserable," Abraham Lincoln, *Lincoln: Speeches and Writings 1832–1858,* ed. Don E. Fehrenbacher (New York: Literary Classics of the United States, 1989), 69.

Page 10, "Today I am speaking of," Jeffrey R. Holland, "Like a Broken Vessel," *Ensign,* November 2013.

Page 10, "Though we may feel," Holland, "Like a Broken Vessel"; emphasis added.

Page 13, "Friendship is born," C. S. Lewis, *The Four Loves* (New York: Harcourt Brace, 1960), 78.

CHAPTER 2
"O GOD, WHERE ART THOU?"

Page 16, "the arid pain of total," Andrew Solomon, *The Noonday Demon: An Atlas of Depression* (New York: Scribner, 2001), 19.

Pages 18–20, Dr. Louise Jorgensen has a PhD in counseling from Oregon State University and post-graduate training at the Harvard-affiliated Benson-Henry Institute for Mind Body Medicine.

Pages 21–22, "so severe that I simply could not," Robert L. Millet, "Starving Our Doubts and Feeding Our Faith," *Religious Educator* 11, no. 2 (2010): 105–9.

Pages 24–25, "telling your story," Lissa Rankin, "The Healing Power of Telling Your Story," *Psychology Today,* November 27, 2012, https://www .psychologytoday.com/blog/owning-pink/201211/the-healing-power -telling-your-story. Accessed December 12, 2017.

CHAPTER 3
THE STORM CLOUD OF STIGMA

Page 37, 350 million people worldwide, see Graham Thornicroft et al., "Undertreatment of people with major depressive disorder in 21 countries," *The British Journal of Psychiatry,* December 2016, http://bjp.rcpsych .org/content/early/2016/11/16/bjp.bp.116.188078/full-text.pdf+html. Accessed December 12, 2017.

Page 37, "The experience of social rejection," Michael Friedman, "The Stigma of Mental Illness Is Making Us Sicker," *Psychology Today,* May 13, 2014, https://www.psychologytoday.com/blog/brick-brick/201405/the -stigma-mental-illness-is-making-us-sicker. Accessed December 12, 2017.

Page 45, "Where can I turn," Emma Lou Thayne, "Where Can I Turn for Peace?" *Hymns* (Salt Lake City: The Church of Jesus Christ of Latter-day Saints, 1985), no. 129.

Page 46, "The bleakest time," Emma Lou Thayne, "Search for inner peace is universal," *Church News,* December 29, 2001.

Page 46, "Sitting at my makeshift desk," Thayne, "Search for inner peace is universal."

Page 48, "Parable of the Bicycle," Stephen E. Robinson, *Believing Christ* (Salt Lake City: Deseret Book, 1992), 30–33.

Page 49, release of a website, https://www.lds.org/mentalhealth. Accessed December 12, 2017.

CHAPTER 4
TOXIC PERFECTIONISM

Page 52, published my first book, Jane Clayson Johnson, *I Am a Mother* (Salt Lake City: Deseret Book, 2007).

Page 53, "of living an inauthentic life," Gordon Flett et al., "The Destructiveness of Perfectionism Revisited," *Review of General Psychology,* Vol. 18 (3), September 2014, 163.

Page 53, "I have been learning," Flett et al., "Destructiveness of Perfectionism," 156.

Page 55, "It will be an even better year," Cecil O. Samuelson, "Be Ye Therefore Perfect," BYU Devotional, September 6, 2011; emphasis added.

Page 55, "What I now say in no way," Jeffrey R. Holland, "Be Ye Therefore Perfect—Eventually," *Ensign,* November 2017; emphasis added.

Page 59, "If sometimes the harder you try," Jeffrey R. Holland, "The Inconvenient Messiah," *Ensign,* February 1984.

Pages 60–61, "Brothers and sisters, every one," Holland, "Be Ye Therefore Perfect—Eventually."

Page 63, "The term *perfect* was translated," Russell M. Nelson, "Perfection Pending," *Ensign,* November 1995; emphasis in original.

Page 68, "a family of four lovely," Gary L. Stevenson, "The Knowledge of a Savior," BYU Devotional, May 5, 2017, https://www.lds.org/prophets -and-apostles/unto-all-the-world/the-knowledge-of-a-savior?lang=eng &clang=pes. Accessed December 13, 2017.

Page 69, "We all have an innate desire," Janet Scharman, "Seeking Perfection without Being a Perfectionist," in *Virtue and the Abundant Life: Talks from the 2010 BYU Symposium,* ed. Lloyd D. Newell (Provo, UT: BYU Religious Education), 282–83.

Page 73, "We found that the more," Daniel K Judd, "New Creatures in Christ," BYU Easter Conference, March 25, 2016, 10; copy in author's possession.

Pages 73–74, "Our only hope for true perfection," Holland, "Be Ye Therefore Perfect—Eventually."

CHAPTER 5
KIDNAPPED SOULS: YOUNG PEOPLE AND DEPRESSION

Page 75, "depression is something different," Jeanne Segal and Melinda Smith, "Parent's Guide to Teen Depression: Recognizing the Signs and Symptoms and Helping Your Child," https://www.helpguide.org/articles /depression/parents-guide-to-teen-depression.htm. Accessed December 19, 2017.

Page 79, 31.9 percent of teens, "Prevalence of Any Anxiety Disorder among Adolescents," https://www.nimh.nih.gov/health/statistics/any-anxiety -disorder.shtml. Accessed July 19, 2018.

Page 80, A 2012 study, Andrea L. Barrocas et al., "Rates of Nonsuicidal Self-Injury in Youth: Age, Sex, and Behavioral Methods in a Community Sample," *Pediatrics,* 130 (1), July 2012, 39–45.

Page 89, "Everyone might not land," Jeff Lindeman, "Jeff's Story," speech to teammates, 6; copy in author's possession.

CHAPTER 6
CALLED TO SERVE, CALLED TO STRUGGLE: MISSIONARIES AND DEPRESSION

Pages 94–95, "expected to devote," "Your Calling," in *Missionary Handbook* (Salt Lake City: The Church of Jesus Christ of Latter-day Saints, 2010), https://www.lds.org/languages/eng/content/manual/missionary -handbook/your-calling. Accessed December 19, 2017.

Page 95, Music listening is restricted, "Missionary Conduct: Music," in *Missionary Handbook.*

Page 95, Headphones are not, "Missionary Conduct: Television, Radio, Movies, Videos, DVDs, Internet," in *Missionary Handbook.*

Page 109, One report from 2014, T. S. Drake and M. L. Drake, "Emotional factors affecting the physical diagnosis in the early release of young missionaries," proceedings from 2014 Association of Mormon Counselors and Psychotherapists (AMCAP) Convention, Salt Lake City, UT, unpublished conference presentation.

Page 109, a major 2015 study, Kristine Doty et al., "Return with Trauma: Understanding the Experiences of Early Returned Missionaries," *Issues in Religion and Psychotherapy* 37 (1), Article 9, 33–45.

Pages 109–10, "we want everyone," Jeffrey R. Holland, "Elder Holland's Counsel for Early Returned Missionaries," https://www.lds.org/media -library/video/2016–05–012-elder-hollands-counsel-for-early-returned -missionaries?lang=eng. Accessed December 19, 2017.

Pages 110–11, 73 percent of the participants, Doty et al., "Return with Trauma," 41. All of the statistics in the paragraph are cited from this source.

Page 111, "I went back to Provo," Doty et al., "Return with Trauma," 41.

Page 111, "The mission president phoned," Doty et al., "Return with Trauma," 41.

Page 111, "I think the hardest," Doty et al., "Return with Trauma," 41.

CHAPTER 7
NOT JUST THE BABY BLUES: POSTPARTUM DEPRESSION

Page 119, "the highest and noblest," Russell M. Nelson, "Our Sacred Duty to Honor Women," *Ensign,* May 1999.

Page 119, "There is eternal influence," Julie B. Beck, "Mothers Who Know," *Ensign,* November 2007.

Page 120, as many as one in five, "Depression Among Women," https://www.cdc.gov/reproductivehealth/depression/index.htm. Accessed December 19, 2017.

Page 120, more women will develop, "How Many Women Really Get PPD," http://www.postpartumprogress.com/how-many-women-get-postpartum-depression-the-statistics-on-ppd. Accessed July 20, 2018.

Page 121, "All women receiving," Ruta Nonacs, in "How Many Women Really Get PPD."

Page 126, "If you think women," Katherine Stone, "6 Surprising Symptoms of Postpartum Depression and Anxiety," June 21, 2012, http://www.postpartumprogress.com/6-surprising-symptoms-of-postpartum-depression-and-anxiety. Accessed December 19, 2017.

Page 127, A study published in, "Post-Up Study: Postpartum Depression Screening in Well-Child Care and Maternal Outcomes," *Pediatrics,* 140 (4), October 2017.

Page 128, "For a woman with," Katherine Stone, "On Postpartum Depression and Insomnia," October 7, 2010; http://www.postpartumprogress.com/on-ppd-and-insomnia. Accessed December 19, 2017.

Page 134, "depression, anxiety, and other," Wendy Leonard, "Utah hospital now screens all new moms for depression," *Deseret News,* November 12, 2017, https://www.deseretnews.com/article/900003913/utah-hospital-now-screens-all-new-moms-for-depression.html. Accessed December 19, 2017.

CHAPTER 8
"AGITATED HORROR AND RELENTLESS DESPAIR": SUICIDAL DEPRESSION

Page 137, "Shalese returned," https://www.heraldextra.com/lifestyles/announcements/obituaries/shalese-black/article_2d6da080-f1ea-5e39-978e-3c805119ac5b.html. Accessed July 19, 2018.

Page 139, "Suicidal depression involves," Kay Redfield Jamison, "To Know Suicide," *New York Times,* August 15, 2014.

Page 141, "The fact that our," although this quote is often attributed to C. S. Lewis, a direct reference to it cannot be found. It is likely, however, that he agreed with the sentiment, as he did say this: "If I find in myself a desire which no experience in this world can satisfy, the most probable explanation is that I was made for another world" (*Mere Christianity,* paperback edition [New York: Harper Collins, 1952], 136–37).

Page 141, more than 44,000, American Foundation for Suicide Prevention, https://afsp.org/about-suicide/suicide-statistics/. Accessed December 19, 2017. The remaining statistics in the table on page 142 are cited from this source, except as indicated.

Page 142, There was a 28 percent increase, *Time* magazine, June 18, 2018.

Page 142, A 70 percent increase in suicide, *Time* magazine, June 18, 2018.

Pages 143–44, "Every one of us has family members," Dale G. Renlund, "Understanding Suicide," https://www.lds.org/get-help/suicide/videos ?lang=eng. Accessed July 2, 2018.

Page 144, "Education is more than," George H. Brimhall, in Mary Jane Woodger and Joseph H. Groberg, *From the Muddy River to the Ivory Tower: The Journey of George H. Brimhall* (Provo: Brigham Young University, 2010), 47.

Page 144, "I know of no single," Heber J. Grant, in Woodger and Groberg, *From the Muddy River,* 198.

Page 145, "members of his family," in Woodger and Groberg, *From the Muddy River,* 203.

Page 145, "Is there anything I should know," John A. Widtsoe, in Woodger and Groberg, *From the Muddy River,* 204–5.

Page 145, "Certainly this was a very," Franklin S. Harris, in Woodger and Groberg, *From the Muddy River,* 205.

Pages 145–46, "It must be a source," George Albert Smith, in *Tributes to George H. Brimhall* (n.p.: Alsina Elizabeth Brimhall Holbrook Family, 1988), 394–95.

Page 146, "I am sure the man was," James E. Talmage, in Woodger and Groberg, *From the Muddy River,* 204.

Pages 147–48, "It's completely safe, completely safe," Dale G. Renlund, "Talking about Suicide," https://www.lds.org/get-help/suicide/videos ?lang=eng. Accessed July 2, 2018.

Page 156, 60 percent of LGB teens had reported feeling "so sad or helpless," L. Kann, E. O. Olsen, T. McManus et al., "Sexual Identity, Sex of Sexual Contacts, and Health-Related Behaviors Among Students in Grades 9–12—United States and Selected Sites, 2015," Morbidity and Mortality Weekly Report, August 12, 2016, http://dx.doi.org/10.15585/mmwr .ss6509a1. Accessed July 19, 2018.

Page 159, "I bear witness of that day," Jeffrey R. Holland, "Like a Broken Vessel," *Ensign,* November 2013.

CHAPTER 9

I JUST WANT TO HELP: FOR FAMILIES AND FRIENDS

Page 162, "ultimately eclipses the capacity," Andrew Solomon, *The Noonday Demon: An Atlas of Depression* (New York: Simon and Schuster, 2001), 15.

Pages 163–64, "Early in our marriage," "Mormons and Mental Illness: Spousal Support," ByCommonConsent.com, December 7, 2005, https:// bycommonconsent.com/2005/12/07/mormons-and-mental-illness -spousal-support/. Accessed December 19, 2017.

Page 165, "Depression is a disease," Andrew Solomon, "Depression is a disease of loneliness," AndrewSolomon.com, August 16, 2014, http:// andrewsolomon.com/articles/depression-is-a-disease-of-loneliness/. Accessed December 19, 2017.

Page 166, "When things first started," "Mormons and Mental Illness: Spousal Support."

Page 168, "Caregivers who pay attention," National Alliance on Mental Illness, "Taking Care of Yourself," https://www.nami.org/Find-Support /Family-Members-and-Caregivers/Taking-Care-of-Yourself. Accessed December 19, 2017.

CHAPTER 10
THE LOWER LIGHTS: A STEWARDSHIP OF HELP AND HOPE

Page 180, approximately one in five, "The State of Mental Health in America," http://www.mentalhealthamerica.net/issues/state-mental-health -america. Accessed December 19, 2017.

Page 181, "Faith communities fail to," Diana Garland, in Rick Nauert, "Mental Illness Nearly Invisible in Many Churches," https://psychcentral .com/news/2011/06/23/mental-illness-nearly-invisible-in-many -churches/27191.html. Accessed December 19, 2017. See also Edward B. Rogers, Matthew Stanford, and Diana R. Garland, "The effects of illness on families within faith communities," *Mental Health, Religion & Culture,* 15 (3), May 25, 2011, 301–13.

Page 182, "lives in invisible wheelchairs," Andrew Solomon, *The Noonday Demon: An Atlas of Depression* (New York: Simon and Schuster, 2001), 162.

Page 183, "The Savior is telling us," Thomas S. Monson, "What Have I Done for Someone Today?" *Ensign,* November 2009.

Page 183, "Let our hearts and hands," Dieter F. Uchtdorf, "'You Are My Hands,'" *Ensign,* May 2010.

Pages 183–184, "Among the most painful," Alexander B. Morrison, "Myths about Mental Illness," *Ensign,* October 2005.

Page 184, "All mental illness is," Morrison, "Myths about Mental Illness."

Page 188, "Some people have been," Rob Waller, in "Mental health and the church," *Christianity Today,* April 23, 2010, https://www.christianitytoday .com/article/mental.health.and.the.church/25777.htm. Accessed December 19, 2017.

Pages 193–94, "Many of our brethren and sisters," Brigham Young, as quoted in Gordon B. Hinckley, "'Reach with a Rescuing Hand,'" *Ensign,* November 1996.

Page 194, "I am proud to be able to say," Beulah Clayson, personal journal, in author's possession.

Page 194, "I am grateful that those days," Hinckley, "'Reach with a Rescuing Hand.'"

Page 195, "Brightly Beams Our Father's Mercy," Philip Paul Bliss, "Brightly

Beams Our Father's Mercy," *Hymns* (Salt Lake City: The Church of Jesus Christ of Latter-day Saints, 1985), no. 335.

CHAPTER 11
"THE MOST POWERFUL MEDICINE ON EARTH"

Page 197, "Telling your story," Lissa Rankin, "The Healing Power of Telling Your Story," *Psychology Today*, November 27, 2012; emphasis added, https://www.psychologytoday.com/blog/owning-pink/201211/the -healing-power-telling-your-story. Accessed January 14, 2018.

Page 198, Gordon B. Hinckley quote, see, for example, Gordon B. Hinckley, "The Marvelous Foundation of Our Faith," *Ensign*, November 2002.

Page 199, "By seeing how many kinds," Andrew Solomon, *The Noonday Demon: An Atlas of Depression* (New York: Scribner, 2001), 429.

Page 200, "depression will only intensify," Solomon, *Noonday Demon*, 453.

Page 200, "recognize that the fire," Alexander B. Morrison, *Valley of Sorrow: A Layman's Guide to Understanding Mental Illness* (Salt Lake City: Deseret Book, 2003), 133.

INDEX

NOTES

NOTES

NOTES

NOTES

NOTES

NOTES

NOTES

NOTES

2.19